SEA, IT'S HAPPENING

A Compilation of Environmental and Sustainability
Education Strategies Infused Across
the K-12 Curriculum

By
Joseph J. Soporowski, Ph.D.

SEA, It's Happening
A Compilation of Environmental and Sustainability Education
Strategies Infused Across the K-12 Curriculum

Printed in the United States of America

ISBN-13: 978-1-7982-4926-0

Sustainable Education Associates, LLC
PO Box 398
Normandy Beach, NJ 08739-0398
seayourfuture@gmail.com
www.seayourfuture.net

Acknowledgments

There exists a select group of people who understand that knowledge is power. Knowledge allows for citizens to make good choices. It protects us from those that would otherwise capitalize on our ignorance and cause us harm. It shields us from oppression, and enables our personal and professional growth.

Through the tireless dissemination of knowledge this admirable assemblage of individuals strives to improve the lives of our children and the health of our society. They are experts in motivation, encouragement, training, and preparation. They provide today's youth with the tools and skills needed for meeting the challenges that the next generation will inevitably face.

I refer, of course, to the teachers of today who believe in their students' ability to shape the world of tomorrow. Our educators have dedicated themselves to the most sacred of causes, and this book is dedicated to them. I pray they will be successful in their efforts, for it is teachers who hold the key to a sustainable future.

Table of Contents

Introduction and How to Use This Book

If you willfully choose to ignore science, insist that the way you learned is the only way that our children will learn, or consciously refuse to accept that our world is facing an environmental crisis, then I suggest you read no further. I am confident that doing so will only result in your frustration. That being said, this book is intended to help educators create an opportunity for our children to have a sustainable future. It is my honor and pleasure to be working with those of you that are still reading!

My name is Joseph Soporowski. I began my career as an environmental scientist. It was an exciting privilege to be exposed to many diverse environmental issues, the challenging problems they posed, and the innovative solutions developed and implemented in order to solve them. I served as a faculty member for the Rutgers University Department of Environmental Sciences, Research Scientist for the New Jersey Department of Environmental Protection, Manager of Air Quality for the State of Arizona, and Associate with several major environmental consulting firms.

After nearly eight years serving in the environmental field, I felt a strong desire to teach at the high school level and jumped head first into secondary education. I loved it! I taught high school chemistry and physics, and even coached baseball and basketball. I couldn't believe I was getting paid for doing something so enjoyable and rewarding. The next fifteen years went by in a blink. I eventually became an educational administrator, and although I missed working directly with the students, I did find the position to be extremely rewarding. I certainly would have been proud to continue in that capacity and eventually retire as a public-school employee, however, I believe everyone has a calling, and in order to achieve true success, a person needs only to find out what that is and answer the call. I knew there was still something else I was supposed to do.

It required nearly 25 years of unintentional preparation, yet when I look back on my life, it all makes sense. With a strong background in both environmental science and academia it is only natural that I currently assist teachers with the process of infusing environmental education into their instruction. In 2016, I began training teachers of all disciplines and grade levels as to the fundamentals of environmental science. The goal of this effort was to promote eco-literacy among the educators so that they would be capable of identifying "infusion points" in their curricula and incorporating relevant environmental issues into their lessons.

I believe by trade most teachers are naturally creative and there is no need to purchase someone else's commercial product or rewrite any existing curricula. I've always operated off the "teach a man to fish" concept. Just provide teachers with the basic environmental background that they will need and allow them to do their thing. In my first book, *Sustainable Education – A Simplistic Strategy For Infusing Environmental Education Into America's Schools*, I provide a brief but comprehensive overview of the major environmental issues. The primer examines the concept of a sustainable society and outlines a very simplistic strategy that all teachers, regardless of grade level or subject area, can use in order to prepare the eco-literate leaders of tomorrow.

We all know that the key to successful learning is motivation. As you will see by the compilation of teacher-developed learning scenarios contained in *SEA – It's Happening*, infusing the issues associated with environmental science and sustainability into your instruction will provide all the motivation your students will ever need to meet their curricular goals. Doing so will make your subject material more relevant to your students' lives and they will want to learn. Today's youth is well aware of the problems that their generation is facing, certainly more aware than most of us were. Don't take my word for it. Ask them.

Becoming eco-literate and infusing environmental science into your teaching is easier than you think. It can be accomplished in any course and almost any lesson. Since establishing Sustainable Education Associates, I have worked with thousands of teachers, and literally traveled the world in search of innovative ways that environmental education has been incorporated into the learning process. I am pleased to say that we, as global educators, are well on our way to developing eco-literate leaders capable of creating a truly healthy planet and sustainable future.

SEA – It's Happening is a compilation of representative samples of activities, projects, presentations, lessons, etc. from a wide variety of grade levels and content disciplines. This book recounts actual scenarios developed and implemented by outstanding teachers just like you. The one thing that all of these heroes have in common is that they are all eco-literate. Some already possessed an environmental background; some participated in one of our sustainable education presentations, workshops, or seminars; some read *Sustainable Education*; and some just did ten minutes of research on their smartphones. I'm not kidding!

I hope that you will be able to read the entire book, as it is important to realize that sustainability education is everyone's job. However, for ease of reference, I have organized this compilation of work into several chapters of related topic disciplines should you wish to take an immediate look at what other teachers that share your area of expertise have been doing.

I consider every teacher who agreed to anonymously share his or her creative work a true educational leader and an inspiration to us all. I am confident that you will enjoy these incredible success stories that demonstrate how simple and effective infusing environmental education into the instruction can be. I hope that you will soon be joining this incredible grassroots movement as it steers our society and the next generation toward a sustainable future. I look forward to learning about your inspirational work in the field of sustainable education!

Chapter 1 – Saving Lives

I have served as a Jersey Shore Lifeguard since the late seventies. Even when working full-time for governmental agencies, environmental engineering firms, colleges, public school districts, and now with Sustainable Education Associates, I have always found a way to "keep my feet in the sand." The full account of what brings me back season after season is a story for another time. However, one of the most obvious reasons I return happens to be the amazing people that I meet from all walks of life.

Refreshingly, I have found that very few people bring their "troubles" to the beach. There are, of course, the typical pleasantries but conversations range from the absurdly hilarious to the gravely serious and cover topics addressing anything from daily routines to world politics. Hidden among all of those encounters is the recurring truth of just how wonderful our world is. However, at the shore, it seems unthinkable to imagine our way of life gone forever rendering the topic of sustainability a discussion that one rarely hears at the beach.

Craig has guarded with me for several years. He is a twenty-three-year-old recent college graduate, a terrific young man, and comes from a very affluent family. His father runs a successful business and hopes for Craig to someday take over the company. Many would say that Craig has it made because he has a lucrative career and the perfect life just waiting for him. However, he sees things a little differently. Since graduating from college a few years ago, Craig has spent most of his time in Nicaragua working as a surfing guide and videographer. I know what you're thinking, "Lazy Spoiled Kid," right? I might have thought the same thing had I not sat next to him on that lifeguard stand. I've watched him grow throughout his high school and college years. I've seen how his values became ingrained into his soul. I know how much he loves his life and the world around him. I've never seen him angry or wearing anything but a smile. He has no political agenda. In fact, he doesn't seem to care about politics at all. Yet something he said this summer resonates in my mind. When I asked him what he plans to do when he is my age, he responded, "The world isn't going to be the same when I'm your age."

Please read Craig's response again and reflect on it for a moment. He is not lazy. He is not looking for the easy way out. He is simply making a well-educated decision based on the information and options available to him. For those of you that believe Craig is an anomaly, think again. Our children know that our way of life is not sustainable and they are beginning to make their voices heard. Young people across the globe are rising up, questioning their politicians, challenging the financial giants, and demanding change because they understand the problems they are inheriting and they are not happy (Aronoff, K., 2019).

We are in the midst of an environmental crisis but many of us don't speak of it because it is an uncomfortable topic. Some people will discredit scientific fact in order to deny its existence. Creating a sustainable society requires sacrifice. The leaders of our society have, and continue to avoid addressing the problem. Should we congratulate them as we are now on the verge of successfully passing the burden onto our children?

The promises made to us by our parents did, for the most part, come true. If you worked hard in school, you could get a good-paying job and retire to enjoy the bounties of this world. At the time of this writing, my wife and I are fortunate enough to be spending considerable time abroad and in the United States, experiencing many fascinating places, cultures, and natural beauty. We are reaping the benefits of living "The American Dream." However, this is today and tomorrow may not hold the same promise for our children.

Will that American Dream be a reality for the next generation? What awaits our children in a world where resources are becoming depleted? What will happen to the human population when ecosystem collapse eradicates many of the species we depend on for our survival? How will the next generation power its society when fossil fuels are no longer available or cause air and water pollution to reach life threatening levels? It is a fact that one hundred years ago there were approximately 2 billion people on this planet and now there are over 7.5 billion (www.census.gov/popclock/). Realize, however, that the amount of fresh water on our Earth has not changed over that time span. It does not take a Ph.D. in environmental science to realize that simply due to exponential population growth, we will soon have a global water crisis on our hands. Please note that I have not even mentioned climate change. I refrained from doing so because there are people that still chose not to accept that human activities are resulting in unnatural variations of our planet's climate and this is merely one aspect of environmental degradation that future generations will have to deal with.

Obviously, my generation has failed young people like Craig. Not only because we are poised to leave them with a society and planet that cannot provide them with the same opportunities and experiences that we enjoyed, but because we have not owned up to our mistakes, and have not yet embraced the need to make sustainability a practice in every aspect of our children's education.

The truth is that we can still make things right and today's educators hold the key to our success. In my educational primer, *Sustainable Education – A Simplistic Strategy For Infusing Environmental Education Into America's Schools*, I outlined a very simplistic and instructor-friendly strategy for teachers of all subjects and grade levels to infuse environmental science into their instruction. The goal of this effort is to prepare eco-literate leaders capable of paving the way to a truly healthy planet and sustainable future.

Since its publication, thousands of teachers across the country have been hard at work incorporating environmental education into their curricula and making core content topics more interesting for their students by demonstrating the relevance to their lives and the future success of our species. In other words, these teachers are answering that age-old question that all educators have heard time and time again, "When am I ever going to use this?" The answer to that question is, of course, right now! For those of you who have read *Sustainable Education*, already teaching sustainability in your classroom, or just want to know a little more about what might be the most important educational movement of our time, allow me to share a brief story that is typical of an educator discovering the power of promoting eco-literacy.

Jay is also a lifeguard at the Jersey Shore. Unlike Craig, he has followed a more traditional path in life. In his early 30s, Jay is an accomplished high school physical education instructor and athletic coach. We have known each other for many years and when I first explained the concept of sustainability education to Jay, he smiled and said that he doesn't have to worry about that because he teaches physical education, which has nothing to do with environmental science. I will spare you the discussion that ensued, however, I will share with you the gist of a letter that Jay received nearly one year later, and after he attended one of our sustainability education workshops. In the letter, the mother of one of his pupils commended him for, "Opening her son's and his parents' eyes to some of the environmental issues that face our society." She went on to say that she has never seen her son so enthusiastic about anything before and he plans to investigate a career in green technologies.

Jay shared this letter with me and told me that he never dreamed he could make such a big difference with such little effort. My response was simple and to the point.

I said, "Don't underestimate your impact just because the task of infusing environmental education was easy. The fact is you could have completely ignored our advice and taught your material as you have in the past. No one would have realized or noticed the missed opportunity. You are a hero just for trying. Imagine if all teachers did what you did." Jay smiled and said, "If all teachers did this, our kids just might have the chance to enjoy what we enjoy." Okay, so what incredible thing did Jay do that was so "life altering"? When you realize how simple the process is, you may run to your school administrators and ask, "Why aren't we all doing this?"

As part of Jay's school district's physical education curriculum, he needed to teach his students about drug addiction and how people with such an affliction can be helped. He simply made an analogy between how our society is addicted to fossil fuels (oil, coal, etc.) in the same way that people can become addicted to illegal drugs. The students discussed how addicts crave the physical "high" that they get from drugs and compared that to the economic "high" our society gets from using fossil fuels. In both instances, people want more and more and are unwilling and oftentimes, unable to change their practices. Just as there are extremely dangerous ramifications of using drugs, there are also serious and negative consequences associated with using fossil fuels.

Isn't it odd that our society has very little issue explaining to our children the problems associated with drug use but when it comes to relying on fossil fuels, the consequences aren't portrayed to be so dire? One student had the courage to say, "Yeah, but some people don't want you to think about the bad side of using fossil fuels just like a drug dealer doesn't want you to think about the bad side of using drugs." Pretty astute for a high school kid, don't you think? Jay's students became engrossed in a higher-level discussion involving not only the required core content of drug addiction but also the environmental issue of renewable verses non-renewable energy sources.

Jay explained a drug addict's need to go through "withdrawal" in order to break the addiction cycle and get back to living a healthy and productive life. It did not take the students long to make the analogy to our society's dependence on fossil fuels and why transitioning to renewable energy sources is such a difficult process. The students concluded that we, as a society, must go through a similar withdrawal and that means sacrifice. They returned home with an understanding of why people may not be willing to accept scientific findings. Like the scientific facts associated with climate change, that information may support conclusions that most people simply do not want to face and so choose to ignore. Give the students credit for realizing that regardless of any refusal to accept the truth, these issues will not simply "go away."

Jay covered his material as required but he made it more interesting for his students by demonstrating the relevance to their lives. Do you think they will ever forget that lesson? They certainly did not fall asleep in class and may now understand why unscrupulous people might try to use certain terms and catch phrases intended to mislead them. Just as we want our children to say no to drugs, Jay's students, and in some cases, their parents will be able to say no to climate change deniers explaining, "Sorry, I know that using the term 'clean coal' is as silly as saying 'healthy poison.' I'm not that gullible." The rest, as they say, is history.

Jay knocked it out of the park! By simply reading *Sustainable Education* and attending one of our workshops, Jay became eco-literate enough to change the lives of over 100 students and many of their parents in one lesson. The best part is that he did this with almost no additional preparation. Imagine if every teacher did this. Perhaps Craig and those like him would have a more optimistic vision for the future. Don't we at least owe our children a sustainable education? Lifeguards save lives. In a way, aren't all teachers lifeguards?

Chapter 2 – Is Everything Okay?

One of the most common questions we are asked when a school district contacts Sustainable Education Associates for professional development or assistance with their "green" initiatives is, "Isn't this really for our Science Department?" The answer is, "Yes, but it's equally important for your English Department, your Math Department, your Language Arts Department, etc." The truth is sustainability education is everyone's job!

I sometimes begin our introductory presentations with a slide displaying two pictures side by side. One is a nighttime photo of our Earth's surface from an aircraft on a clear night. The other is an image of a person's back suffering from some type of skin disease. I ask the participants to simply make a comment on what they see. The majority of individuals state that the picture of the Earth is beautiful and the one depicting diseased skin is unpleasant. However, there always seems to be a few participants that point out a stark similarity. They state that both pictures portray a problem. Quite right. A dermatologist would be quick to identify that the pustules on the person's back are an indication of a disease. However, what would a "doctor of planets" say about our Earth while observing pockets of light littering its nighttime surface? Would not the lights from our cities be an indication that our planet is suffering from some type of infection?

I think the answers depend on one's point of view and the values inherent in each of us. Most of us are conditioned to be repulsed by skin disease but have been born and raised in a society where lights represent progress and are viewed as beautiful. You are not an enemy of the environment if you look out an airplane window at the lights below and see beauty. However, the next time you are flying at night, you may also be able to see the beast. Like a virus spreading on a person's skin, human beings are spreading across our Earth. A viral infection is not sustainable. Either the infection is eliminated or the host organism dies. Please do not think that I am comparing human beings to a virus, quite the contrary. Instead, I am attempting to point out that unlike a virus, we have the dignity of choice. We can choose to live in a way that avoids depletion of natural resources in order to maintain an ecological balance. We do not have to overrun our planet and become extinct. That should be our goal, to live sustainably.

Achieving this goal is easier said than done. A very intelligent person once said, "Until we agree that our species must live in a sustainable manner, we will continue heading down a very dangerous path." The unfortunate truth is that we do not all share the same viewpoint when it comes to our role on this planet. Some of us believe that human beings are the master species and have the right to transform the Earth as they see fit. These individuals will argue that human ingenuity will be able to overcome any negative consequences resulting from our actions. For example, we may create air, water, and soil pollution, however our technology will provide a means to solve these problems. Others maintain that humans must not use our technology to alter our environment in any way other than what nature has intended. Hundreds of years ago, many of the Native Americans held this worldview as sacred. Still others feel that the role of human beings lies somewhere in the middle, believing that people may make the world the way they want it to be but then have the responsibility of restoring the environment anytime it has been disrupted as a result of our activities (Noblet, C., Lindenfeld, L., & Anderson, M. 2013).

I think it is safe to say that we really can't expect to go back to living in caves and wearing animal skins, nor can we just continue to ravage the planet and hope that future generations find ways to correct the mess that we will leave for them. Things have already progressed as far as they have and if we put our minds to it and dedicate ourselves to the cause, just maybe we can sustain this way of life for many generations to come. However, in order to do that, we must first identify the challenges we face, and understand the principles of environmental science that will help us overcome them. In my educational primer, *Sustainable Education*, I outline and examine the myriad of environmental problems facing future societies. I will only summarize some of the major issues here.

Let's start with overpopulation and resource depletion. Carrying capacity is a term scientists use to describe the maximum population of a species that an environment can support. Ever since human beings discovered fossil fuels, they have been able to engage in activities that transform the planet to suit their specific needs and support a population that far exceeds the carrying capacity for the species. One hundred years ago there were approximately two billion people on the planet. Increasing at an exponential rate, our population has nearly tripled since then as we have already surpassed 7.5 billion (Daily, G. C., & Ehrlich, P. R., 1994).

We must recognize that there are no supply ships coming from other planets to replace the resources that this soaring population is demanding. Even if one chooses to ignore the devastation that we are causing to the ecosystems that we rely on, common sense dictates that it is only a matter of time before the resources we rely on are used up and we begin fighting among ourselves for the little that remain. We refer to this scenario as resource depletion.

The Earth has remarkable abilities to cleanse itself. Consider the miracle we call rain. As polluted as it might be, when solutions evaporate, the water they contain is returned to the atmosphere in pure form. Certain plants absorb pollutants from the environment, process the contaminants, and return them to the soil as nutrients. Since grade school, we have learned how plants can purify the air. However, we are polluting our environment at such an incredible rate that we are overwhelming these regenerative services that nature provides us with for free (Prugh, T. et. al., 1999). In addition, our society is developing new substances to which our planet has never before been exposed. As a result, no natural process exists to break them down and return them to simpler, less harmful materials. In the most basic sense, we are transforming our environment into one that is becoming inhospitable and toxic to entire ecosystems.

Political debates aside, whether human induced or not, our Earth is getting warmer (Finlayson, C. M., 2016). The climates of worldwide biomes are changing. That is a fact. This is resulting in a loss of species. The abundance and diversity of species, also called biodiversity, is like an insurance policy for life on our planet. It is akin to having more than enough employees that are skilled in specific tasks so that even if some leave, the company will still be able to run effectively and efficiently. However, as habitats are being destroyed by human activities, more and more species are being eliminated from the planet. Similar to losing skilled employees in a company, we are losing important species in our ecosystems. Eventually, those ecosystems will collapse, and us with them (Vellend, M. 2017).

We are an unsustainable society but many people fail to recognize this. Our resources are like money in a savings account. If you continue to take cash out at a faster rate than you replenish the account, eventually you will run out. Why is it that this concept is so easy to understand but we have difficulty when it comes to relating it to resources on our planet? The answer most likely lies in the enormity of the situation and the fact that there is a fundamental flaw in our growth-based, economic system.

Imagine you own a company that makes things. It costs money to get the raw materials from the Earth. It costs money to process the raw materials. It costs money to make the things in your factory. It costs money to market and sell your things. The good news is that you make money selling your things and when you subtract how much money you spent from the money you made in the process, you turn a profit. Congratulations, you are a success in our economic society!

Here is the problem. Our Earth is the most unselfish entity that ever existed. Did you notice that you never paid the planet back for what you took from it? Did you pay the Earth for the natural services that it provides every day such as cleaning the air, water, and soil? The answer is no. Our economic system is based on growth but does not take into account that we are degrading the Earth. As "economic capital" increases, "natural capital" decreases. This was not so apparent when we had less than one billion people, but now that we are over 7.5 billion strong, the Earth is starting to show signs that it cannot support our flawed economic systems. If economists continue to exclude the Earth's natural capital and free services from their calculations, we may someday become the wealthiest species to have ever caused its own extinction (Groot, R. D. et. al., 2012).

Many people want to blame their politicians for the problems associated with our unsustainable society. That really isn't logical. In a democracy, elected officials do what people want. Maybe not initially, but over long periods of time, that is what keeps them in office. The big question is, "Do people know or even want what is best for them?" In my initial presentations to teachers, I show them a picture of a young woman sitting at the dinner table. On her right are all types of delicious treats such as fast foods, cakes, candies, and other tasty snacks. On her left are the typical healthy and nutritious food options. The young lady appears to be in good health and most workshop participants expect her to make the better choice and select the healthy food. However, this is America and the choice is up to her. Should she opt for a poor diet, she will need to live with the consequences. That seems fair because she has been taught both at home and in her schooling the value of a healthy diet. However, imagine that her parents failed to address the subject and nutrition was not covered in her formal education. Worst yet, what if such knowledge was intentionally withheld from her or she was provided with misleading information? That would indeed be tragic.

Similarly, infusing environmental concepts into a student's formal education has never been, and is not now mandatory. How then can our voting public be expected to make intelligent decisions when it comes to electing candidates that are champions of a sustainable society? That is where teachers and sustainable education come in. Our educational system must break the cycle that is producing leaders that base their decisions on economic growth, bottom lines, and compliance with outdated expectations. Educational systems instead must make sure that today's youth and tomorrow's decision makers will base their choices on sustainable practices, quality of life, and the needs of future generations. Until that happens, everything is not okay.

Chapter 3 – Great Expectations

Have you ever heard a student ask, "When am I ever going to use this?" That's a silly question. We all have, of course. However, if you are infusing environmental education into your teachings you are able to answer, "right now." One of the biggest knocks on today's educational system is that it is failing to prepare students for the jobs that will be available in the future. Apply just a bit of common sense and one will realize that many of those careers will be in the field of sustainability. Think about it. In order to prolong the functionality of our society, we will need to transition from our growth-based mentality to one that embraces the principles of sustainability. Unfortunately, my generation has proven itself incapable of such a task. However, future generations that include the young teachers of today and their students must be able to do so. They will have no choice.

It's hard for some of us to admit it but most traditional careers will become obsolete in the near future. Our children will be living in "Green" or "Eco-Cities." These communities will be built around principles of sustainability such as renewable energy, mass transit, closed-loop materials cycling, urban agriculture, and innovative concepts such as biomimicry, just to name a few (Vercillo, K., 2012). As educators, we must anticipate what our children will need to know in order for us to prepare them for success.

There are numerous trade schools that prepare students for specific technical and scientific careers in environmental science (Environmental Technology Schools, 2019). However, the truth is that there are many different paths that can lead to jobs in the field of sustainability. These trade schools will certainly produce eco-literate graduates capable of tackling specific environmental problems yet that will not be enough to create an entire sustainable society. To do that, nearly all citizens must attain some level of eco-literacy.

I continue to keep myself immersed in the ground floor of the educational process. I make it a priority to visit and observe schools several times a month just to keep current with what is going on in the classrooms. Here is something that I have observed and I am sure it's taking place all too often. Recognizing the importance of sustainability education, I have noticed that school leaders are working to increase enrollment in courses dedicated to environmental science. You may be saying, "That's good, right?" Although well intentioned, I believe that this practice is actually counterproductive. Analogous to the situation I described involving trade schools, only a select group of individuals actually receive the information that the entire population requires. In fact, a typical comment by school administrators learning of SEA's mission is something like, "We already have an environmental science class for students who are interested in that kind of thing." We must stop teaching environmental science in a silo and perpetuating this feedback loop that fails to produce eco-literate leaders. No matter what the discipline or grade level, I am confident that we are all realizing that the time has finally come when we have to admit that change is necessary, not in how we deliver our instruction but the manner by which we relate the content. It is time to infuse environmental education into our teaching in order to prepare our students for careers of the future.

Common sense dictates that there are always going to be jobs available for those people who know how to fix things that are broken. Well, our planet is in dire need of fixing! Although that isn't good news for us, it certainly is great news for those students who wish to take advantage of career opportunities in sustainability. For this reason alone we should get them ready for the task. The following is just a small sampling of what is coming down the pike and I encourage you to take some time to research this topic on your own. I trust you will be surprised by what you find.

One of the first career opportunities that come to mind when we think of sustainability is the renewable energy field that includes innovative applications such as solar, wind, geothermal, and biomass. There will be a great need for engineers, technicians, and installers. People trained in energy trading and storage, as well as capture and storage of carbon emissions will also be in high demand.

Experts with skills in protecting our valuable resources such as soil, air, and water quality including climate change specialists will play a key role in the success of our society. In the farming and food production industries there will be a rise in "green agriculture jobs" ranging from soil conservation to education and research.

Traditional construction will morph into "green construction" using products that have been manufactured for lower impact on the environment. New architectural design will incorporate innovative concepts such as tiny houses, rooftop agriculture, and independent energy generation. These green buildings will take advantage of closed-looped materials recycling resulting in waste reduction (Wallace, M., 2008).

Language arts and social studies teachers will take solace in knowing that governmental and regulatory administrations will seek qualified individuals capable of developing, writing, and implementing new and appropriate laws. These people will be addressing the issues associated with transitioning our society to one that is completely sustainable. The ability to support and defend one's position will be a crucial skill for non-profit organizations advocating for specific environmental causes. Those choosing to work for private firms will need to understand these laws and regulations to keep their clients in compliance.

Of course, there will always be the hard-core scientists dedicated to research, design, and development. Scientific disciplines in their infancy such as the field of biomimicry will offer incredible opportunities for the progressive thinkers. It's not long before climate science is an everyday word. The field will employ many young scientists set on preventing what was once thought to be the sure demise of our ecosystems. Even controversial practices such as fracking may offer opportunities for innovative problem solvers to perhaps develop methodologies to eliminate the current deficiencies in the process and possibly unlock its full potential.

At the root of many of our environmental problems is overpopulation. Many young minds will be put to the task of developing ethical, moral, and socially acceptable programs aimed at controlling global populations. A major key will be balancing these programs with efficient shifts in resources from one world population to another.

Who can argue that social media specialists will not play an important role in a sustainable future? Social media channels will undoubtedly be the "fire" that spreads eco-literacy throughout the world. It will drive our society to change its harmful growth mentality to one that holds the wellbeing of future generations as its top priority. This kind of "green marketing" will ultimately provide us with an optimistic vision of the future and the motivation to make those dreams a reality (Green Careers, 2010).

I could go on and on, however, it is already obvious that we cannot continue to teach our disciplines as if the world is status quo. Our children need to be prepared for these "green" careers of tomorrow. We must adjust our instructional goals or become obsolete ourselves. Even if not mandated, there is a powerful, determined, and growing grassroots movement whose goal is to infuse environmental education into all aspects of our future leaders' educational experience. One by one, community and school leaders are buying into this concept. Creative teachers are finding innovative ways to infuse environmental education into their daily teaching without disrupting the existing curricular process. Children across the nation are discussing, applying, and practicing their problem-solving skills on real world issues that they find are already a part of their lives.

The following chapters are dedicated to providing a small sampling of what is already being accomplished by teachers just like you. In many of these scenarios I have had the privilege of being an active participant or first hand observer. I have done my best to relay the information accurately and in a manner that is as consistent with the actual events as possible. The experience has solidified my faith in our teachers' ability to create the next generation of eco-literate leaders. I have great expectations!

Where possible, I have attempted to organize the strategies by subject, however as you will see, the infusion of environmental education is taking place at every grade level and in every content discipline. All credit for the ideas, practices, strategies, etc. that will be discussed herein is given to the anonymous, outstanding, dedicated, innovative, and most importantly, caring teachers who generously have shared their success stories with us. Should you have any questions, or wish to learn more about any instructional strategy that is presented in this book, please do not hesitate to contact me for more information.

Chapter 4 – Do The Math

Although I did well in most of my math courses, at least from the grading aspect, I must admit that I detested the subject as a student. To me it just seemed like an endless set of puzzles, procedures, and routine tasks. I often compared my assignments to working on one of those "brainteaser" books like word searches, crosswords, and Sudoku. When I look back, I do feel a bit of regret as I now realize it did not have to be that way.

As a young environmental science student at Rutgers University, I was enrolled in a course entitled *Stream Sanitation.* I will never forget the day that I was wading in a brook and observing the "die-away," the rate of change of concentration, or dilution of a colored test substance introduced upstream by our instructor. All of a sudden, I had a revelation and it hit me like a bolt of lightning. I immediately thought to myself, "This is calculus! Why didn't my teachers ever use this example in class?" Come to think of it, my calculus teachers never made any connections at all to environmental science. Everything seemed backwards and for lack of a better term, I felt betrayed by my instructors. Calculus would have made more sense to me, and perhaps I would have enjoyed studying the subject had my teachers explained why we were learning these mathematical concepts and how they might be used to solve meaningful, real world problems. The truth is that many of my environmental science courses were in a sense, mathematics courses. What a missed opportunity!

There exists a true disconnect between the concepts that we teach in our specific mathematics courses and the real-world situations to which these skills may be applied. I often recount a true story to emphasize this reality. When I first applied to become a high school science teacher through New Jersey's Alternate Route Program, I was initially denied candidacy due to what was termed, "lack of applicable credits." Having earned a doctoral degree in environmental sciences, I found that hard to believe. Upon questioning the Department of Education's decision, I discovered that since the courses I had taken were part of an environmental science curriculum they were not considered applicable to the math, physics, or chemistry certifications. However, as soon as I presented the course syllabi to the admissions evaluators, they immediately applied these courses as higher-level math, physics, and chemistry and accepted every credit. The good news is that I did receive my teaching certificate. However, it is disturbing that, at the time, even our own Department of Education failed to see the relevance of the very core content they were in charge of overseeing.

That was then, this is now. Although not yet mandated, teachers are taking it upon themselves to help their students become more eco-literate by infusing environmental concepts into their teaching. The key is relevance and if there are two aspects of society that youth seem to relate to better than their elders it's technology and sustainability. Let's start by taking a look at how some elementary school teachers are making math more relevant and interesting for their students by connecting their subject content to real world applications.

All little kids seem to enjoy filling things up. They fill up their cereal bowls, toy boxes, Halloween bags, beach pails, etc. Even before we learn how to talk, we learn how to fill things up. For these reasons it is easy to see why the concept of "filling up" is relatable not only to a child but to all of us. However, relevance depends on one's personal viewpoint. It is unlikely that your elementary teachers considered discussing the idea that the Earth is "filling up" with people. Why would they? When you were in grade school there were billions of less people on the planet than there are now. However, as the saying goes, "Kids aren't stupid." Even in the early grade school years, children are aware of the fact that population is becoming a problem. If you don't believe me, just ask a child. You may be surprised by what you hear.

Jen is an elementary school teacher. For one of her math modules, she needed to cover and develop basic graphing skills with her class. After a very brief Internet search on the topic of human population growth, she decided to use the concept as a relevant application for almost all of the core content areas that she was planning to address. In order to meet her goals, she could have simply provided the census data to her students and followed the same instructional strategies that she had done for years. That strategy had always worked for her in the past. Instead, she decided to create a learning environment that allowed her students to first research human population and then engage in higher-order discussions on the topic.

At this point you are saying, "I don't have time for that!" Yes, you do. For Jen, the short amount of time needed to get the students "into it" was obviously worth its weight in gold as the students became enthusiastic about graphing. What Jen found to be most interesting was that the students were concentrating on the actual values and not so much on the graphing techniques. That is, instead of using the data for learning how to graph, they were graphing to understand the data. As any good educator will tell you, the ability of students to apply what they have learned to solve problems is one of the most important goals of education.

Since the students were motivated to see the results of their efforts, they initiated the learning and mastery of the core content became second nature. What exactly did Jen do that was so different?" Actually, she did nothing more than take advantage of three concepts; first, today's youth cares about population growth (relevance); second, work is only work if you don't want to do it (motivation); and third, people understand that "things fill up" (relatable). In short, by infusing environmental science into her instruction, Jen motivated her students by making the learning more relevant and interesting.

Sara put environmental science to work in her third-grade unit on fractions. When the students entered the classroom, they thought that they were in for a treat because cups containing colored candies had been set up on the tables. Warning them not to eat any of the candy, Sara asked her students to observe the mixtures in the containers. She then asked the students to remove just the red candies and put them in a separate cup. She said, "We are going to imagine that the red ones are bad for us and the other colors are fine for us to eat." She then asked the students to place 2 red and 8 non-red candies in a cup. She showed the class how this ratio can be expressed as the fraction 2(red)/10(total) or 2/10 that can be reduced to 1/5. She then told the students that they are to assume that a ratio of 1(red)/5(total) will make a person sick.

Sara asked the students to imagine that there was a barrel of one million candies in front of them and that none of the candies in it were red. She asked, "Who would be willing to eat a scoop?" Almost all of the students raised their hands. She then asked the students to imagine that they were blindfolded and she threw exactly 10 red candies into the barrel and mixed them in. She asked, "Who would be willing to take a scoop now?" After a slight hesitation, nearly all of the hands went up. Sara said, "I thought I told you that the red candies were bad for you." One of the students responded, "Yeah, but it's below the harmful level." That's exactly what he said! In third grade, the students had gotten their first introduction not only to how we measure and report pollution but how we set our threshold standards.

Sara seized this opportunity and before you know it the class was talking about air and water pollution. Sara explained how lead in water is measured in ppm, or parts of lead per one million parts of water. She clearly showed her students that this was nothing more than a very small fraction. Needless to say, the students found this very interesting and the level of engagement was extraordinary.

Sara had the students practice with their fractions by setting up different ratios and reducing them if possible. Before cleaning up for the day, she decided to infuse one more environmental concept by proposing a series of questions. She asked, "How would you remove the red candies from the others if you could not touch them and they were made of metal?" "Use a magnet," was the overwhelming response. "Okay," she asked, "What if the reds were not metal but you had heavy beads that stuck magically to the red candies?" One girl raised her hand and said, "If you shake the candies, the heavy beads will attach to the reds and fall to the bottom. Maybe you can then remove the other colors from the top." Not bad for a third grader. That's how we separate some particulates in our wastewater treatment process.

Remember that the goal was to learn fractions. The objective was certainly met but the students were motivated to learn fractions so that they could apply the concept to solving more relevant problems. Sara made the learning meaningful while increasing the eco-literacy of her students. Do you remember the lesson in which you learned about fractions in grade school? Probably not, but I'll bet that Sara's students will always remember their experience.

Dave, an eighth-grade math teacher, wanted his students to be able to interpret graphical data and draw appropriate conclusions. He thought that this was the perfect opportunity to allow the students to examine the concept of climate change without any outside or biased distractions. He provided his classes with actual National Oceanographic and Atmospheric Administration (NOAA) data on carbon dioxide levels in ppm as well as temperature change since 1960 (US Department of Commerce, & NOAA National Centers for Environmental Information, 2018). The students were given ample time to graph the data and analyze the curves.

Although Dave facilitated and guided the activity, the learning was initiated and driven primarily by the students. After several minutes of analysis one student commented, "How can anyone dispute the conclusion that climate change is occurring?" Dave responded by explaining how he provided the students with only one set of data, and that he would expect them to question a single, outside, informational source. He challenged the class to research and obtain more information for tomorrow and said that they will have time to graph and interpret the data that they uncover.

The next day the evidence poured in and the class soon arrived at its own conclusion. "So," Dave asked, "Do you accept that climate change is occurring?" The response was a resounding, "Yes." "Why?" he asked. The students supported their findings with an analysis of the graphs corresponding to the very data they obtained. What a concept, students researching and using scientific data, applying some basic mathematical graphing skills, and developing their own conclusions. Dave asked, "What is the point of graphing data?" One student said it best; "It makes it easy to see what is happening." Curricular goal met, eco-literacy improved, one step closer to a sustainable education!

Morgan's second grade class had commented on their teacher's new adjustable desk. It allowed her to sit or stand while doing her work. Rather than provide a quick response, Morgan decided to relate several of the upcoming math lessons to the environmental field we call ergonomics. Knowing that the class needed to practice their addition and subtraction skills, she decided to have them perform the same mathematical computations that a professional industrial hygienist does on a daily basis.

The students may not have been so excited had Morgan said, "It's time to add and subtract," but she certainly sparked their interest with her brief introduction to the field of ergonomics, the study of people's efficiency in the workplace (Ergonomics for Schools, 2019). During their introduction to the topic, students were observed examining their own desks and chairs, analyzing the different proportions of their bodies and preparing a myriad of questions for their teacher. Instead of the age-old worksheet of endless problems, Morgan asked the students to add and subtract different values of size and length so that they could actually see and feel the results of their calculations for themselves. Students formed connections between the environment surrounding them and the math problems they were performing.

One boy actually had the courage to say, "I like this better than math." Many of his classmates demonstrated support for his comment. Morgan just smiled. Seems like common sense, right? Of course, but then why don't teachers do this all of the time? The answer is that most teachers are not eco-literate. Not by any fault of their own, they have never had the necessary exposure to environmental science. However, even a brief overview of the most basic environmental issues would enable them to identify appropriate "infusion points" in their curricula where relevant concepts in sustainability could be used to enhance the student learning.

Melissa teaches high school geometry. One day, her students arrived in class and were greeted with the sound of loud highway traffic. Most of them smiled and laughed as they awkwardly found their seats. The sound was so loud that they needed to raise their voices to hear one another. When the bell rang, Melissa hit a key on her laptop and the volume dropped. "Better?" she said. The students nodded in agreement and one asked, "What is that?" Melissa responded, "The sound you are hearing is that of highway noise with a noise barrier in place and what you heard when you first entered is what people deal with living next to a highway that has no barrier." Boy, did she have the students' attention.

Melissa showed the class a brief video on noise barriers. It explained what they are, and how they work (Guidelines On Design of Noise Barriers, 2019). The students immediately made a connection. "Hey, we just did that math in class," said one student. The engineer in the video had explained the application of basic geometric concepts as if the whole point of Melissa's class was to understand noise barriers. Of course, this one environmental area is not the sole purpose of learning geometry, but on this day, points, lines, surfaces, shapes, solids, and angles seemed to be the most important things ever learned.

Melissa designed, developed, and presented the students with a brief activity that engaged them in "modeling" sound as it traveled over the top of differently constructed noise barriers. She explained that there are computer applications that engineers use to perform these analytical problems quicker, however, the students were clearly impressed to see that the very concepts that they were learning in class were the very same procedures that engineers use to solve real world problems. The class concluded with an "exit" activity that asked students what they had learned. One student wrote, "I learned why we need to understand geometry." On the way out the door, a group of students asked Melissa if she could do this again. "Just you wait," she said.

At our introductory presentations to school districts, I often ask, "How many of you know exactly what happens to the water that we flush down the toilet?" I am no longer surprised to find that most people have very little or no idea. I love the reaction that math teachers have to our brief introduction to water and wastewater treatment. The math is everywhere! I won't go into the details of the operations at this time; however, it is quite an interesting process. For this reason, it is very easy to spark student interest. After you get by all of the "yucks" and "ewws" you are usually inundated with enthusiastic questions as the students realize that this process has a very big impact on their lives.

Julie is a high school math teacher who attended one of our introductory workshops. She immediately saw the connection of water and wastewater treatment to algebra and stated that she was confident she would be able to use these concepts to teach a large portion of her course curriculum. She certainly made good on her promise. One day, Julie broke with the regular routine to say to her class, "Okay, we've been learning how to graph, manipulate variables, and solve equations. In the next few days we will learn about an application of these concepts and you will hopefully gain an appreciation for why we are learning algebra in the first place."

The class loved Julie's general introduction to wastewater treatment. The students seemed genuinely fascinated by this everyday process that they had been taking for granted. Although she dedicated an entire class period toward understanding the treatment process, she now had a relevant topic to serve as a reference point for the remainder of the school year. Julie started the students off with some very basic equations of flow. They varied the size of the pipe and calculated the changing flow rates. She added in some area and pressure calculations along with a brief discussion on settling by gravity. Gradually, the process came alive mathematically for her students. Everything was making sense through math. One student commented, "This is like a video game, you can pretty much figure out what is going to happen ahead of time." "You're right," Jen said. She used that statement as a bridge to introduce a video of a treatment plant control room. The operator explained how quantities are measured and calculations performed in "real time" to adjust for changing variables.

You may be thinking, "Isn't this more appropriate for a physics class?" It is equally possible that a physics teacher may think this is more appropriate for an algebra class. The truth is that sustainability education is appropriate in all disciplines. The key is identifying when and where to make the connections. That is, determining the most effective "infusion points." How many of us can recall when we learned a specific concept in algebra class? Probably very few of us will be able to. How many of Julie's students will remember when they learned to apply algebra to wastewater treatment? Probably all.

I mentioned earlier that I truly never understood calculus until I was standing in an actual brook observing the die-away of a test material deposited upstream by one of my college professors. It all made sense to me at that moment as I was now applying my mathematical skills to a relevant real-world scenario. It comforts me to know that more and more teachers are infusing environmental science into their instructional strategies. This is enabling students across the nation to experience that same kind of "aha" moment. In fact, when I heard that Tom was covering air pollution dispersion in his calculus course, I had to come out and visit.

One can say that calculus is the study of continuous change. Tom was determined to demonstrate the necessity for understanding calculus to his students by explaining how pollutants released into our environment move through the air, soil, and water. Tom prepared a mini-lesson for his students focusing on air pollution modeling, measurement techniques, and air quality standards. It was interesting to observe how many students were completely unaware that pollutants in the air could be measured, let alone modeled mathematically.

Employing a basic computer application similar to those used by professional air quality specialists, the students were able to observe how pollutant concentrations change as they move through the air. The students worked with, and applied a myriad of variables that may or may not be able to be controlled by our "real world" production processes that discharge pollutants into the atmosphere. It was refreshing to see and hear the students discussing the importance of variables such as smokestack height, wind speed, wind direction, plume rise, etc. in class. At times, this class closely resembled a team of air pollution engineers evaluating the environmental impacts of a local factory more than it did a group of high school students working on an activity for a mathematics course. Talk about teaching for career and college readiness, this was education at its best. The students were visibly excited, initiating their work, and driving the learning process. They seemed motivated to learn the core content simply because the relevance to the real world and their own lives was so clear.

Tom allowed the students to research air pollution modeling on their smartphones. Students were observed discussing similar work that is performed on a daily basis at NOAA and the United States Environmental Protection Agency (USEPA) (Managing Air Quality - Ambient Air

Monitoring, 2018). Obviously impressed with the quality of the lesson, I asked Tom how much preparation was needed to pull this off. He said that since he considers pollution modeling interesting, brushing up on the topic was not that difficult. Once he found the modeling app that the students would be using, the rest just fell into place. When asked if he would do this again next year he said, "Now that I see how well this worked, I can't imagine doing anything else."

The preceding accounts were just an extremely small but representative sampling of how math teachers across the country are infusing environmental science into their instruction. In almost every instance, student motivation, engagement, content comprehension and retention, along with problem solving skills were reported as exceptional. Furthermore, all of this was accomplished with minimal, if any, additional preparation time and/or financial resources. Regardless of the grade level or subject discipline you teach, if you would like to know more about the first steps necessary for infusing environmental science into your instruction, I invite you to read, *Sustainable Education - A Simplistic Strategy For Infusing Environmental Education Into America's Schools*. If you do the math, it's a no-brainer!

Chapter 5 – A Physical Education

If you think back to the days when you were participating in physical education and health classes in school, we older folks called it "gym," you may fail to initially see the connection to environmental science. However, if you contemplate the relevance you will realize that health and physical education is all about learning to live in harmony with one's physical surroundings or environment. In fact, how can one study physical education without developing a fundamental understanding of the environmental factors that affect our daily lives?

Remember Jay, the physical education teacher that I mentioned in Chapter One? Jay's goal was to familiarize his students with the problems associated with drug addiction and outline the strategies that health professionals use to help people overcome such an affliction. By making an analogy between the way our society is addicted to fossil fuels (oil, coal, etc.) and the way that people can become addicted to drugs, Jay effectively "hooked" his students.

It was interesting how easily the students made the connection between the physical "high" that addicts receive from drugs, and the economic "high" that our society seems to derive from using fossil fuels. The students discussed that in both cases, there exists an uncontrollable craving and people are unwilling and oftentimes, unable to change their self-destructive habits. Students demonstrated an understanding that just as there exist negative consequences associated with drug use, the same can be said about our society's reliance on fossil fuels.

As mentioned earlier, it is strange that our society has very little issue discussing with its children the problems caused by habitual drug use, however, when it comes to relying on fossil fuels, the consequences are not portrayed to be so dire. When one student had the courage to say, "Yeah, but some people don't want you to think about the bad side of using fossil fuels just like a drug dealer doesn't want you to think about the bad side of using drugs," Jay knew he was on to something special.

The fact that Jay's students became engrossed in higher-order discussions involving not only the required core content of drug addiction but also the environmental issue of renewable verses non-renewable energy sources is a testament to his exceptional skills as an educator. When Jay explained how difficult it is for a drug addict to go through "withdrawal" in order to break the addiction cycle and get back to living a healthy and productive life, it did not take his students long to make the analogy to our society's hesitancy to withdraw from its reliance on fossil fuels. They were able to comprehend the reasons for why transitioning to renewable energy sources is so difficult. When the students concluded that we, as a society, must go through a withdrawal process, and that means sacrifice, they were demonstrating the ability to put what they were learning in class to work for the benefit of mankind. Jay had certainly found a way to make a truly positive difference in the lives of his students.

Probably the most rewarding aspect of Jay's effort was the students' ability to "accept" scientific findings. They can no longer be duped by intentionally misleading information or what some have referred to as "alternative facts," especially as it may pertain to the subject of climate change. Jay certainly covered his material but made it more interesting for his students by demonstrating its relevance. There were several parents commenting that their children enthusiastically shared what they had learned with them so it was obvious that Jay was able to educate not only his students but also all those with whom they are associated. Thank you, Jay, for demonstrating the power of a sustainable education.

After attending one of our workshops, Natalie decided to enhance her upcoming unit on body conditioning and strength training. She wanted her students to understand the environmental science behind what they were learning in class. As she had always done in the past, Natalie set up various stations in the weight room with each being designed to target a specific aspect of improving strength and conditioning. Students received specific instructions for each station in the proper use of equipment and how to perform the activity in order to obtain the greatest physical benefit and achieve the maximum positive results.

Over the next several weeks, students were observed perfecting their training skills, improving their overall conditioning, as well as tracking their progress. This was nothing new for Natalie and her students. What was different this time was that she added a brief, 5-minute discussion and/or activity to the beginning of each session addressing the connections between kinesiology and ergonomics so that her students would see the correlation between environmental science and physical fitness. Natalie explained to her students that humans have separated themselves from nature and have, in a sense, created an artificial habitat. This unnatural society creates problems for the human body.

Natalie found interesting ways to connect body movements to the study of a person's efficiency and effectiveness in the work environment. These instructional "spots" included brief videos addressing a diversity of topics ranging from professional sports and performance to work-related injuries and athletic product development. Some students expressed heightened interest when Natalie addressed sports injury management and rehabilitation. Students brought up a plethora of topics such as carpal tunnel syndrome, lifting injuries, careers in physical therapy, etc.

It was obvious that Natalie had taken her unit on strength training to another level. She made it "personal" for her students by demonstrating the relevance not only to improving their own level of physical fitness but how and why the techniques and strategies they were using were developed in the first place. When the unit was completed, I asked Natalie to reflect on the entire experience. She explained that the level of engagement had increased dramatically over past sessions. She said that it seemed as if adding the dynamic of relevance gave the students a purpose for initiating the learning and enthusiastically participating in the physical activity. Natalie added that she never had so many inquiries with regard to possible careers in physical fitness and personal well-being. Perhaps, Natalie answered that age-old question for her students, "Why are we learning this?" Just as I was about to leave, Natalie stopped me and said, "You know, I learned a lot myself. This really is a great way to teach." Enough said!

Walt is an elementary school, physical education teacher who constantly promotes cardiovascular health through exercise. Understanding the importance of lung capacity and recognizing the negative effects that air-borne contaminants (air pollution) can have on the human body, Walt decided to introduce his students to the fundamentals of air pollution.

Using only basic supplies such as a balloon, string, and ruler, Walt developed a clever activity in which his students defined and physically estimated their lung capacity. He explained that performance in sports is linked to how well the body can bring oxygen into the lungs and expel carbon dioxide. Walt said, "The greater a person's lung capacity, the better their body will be able to perform this task." The students immediately made the connection between regular exercise and a person's ability to increase their lung capacity.

Walt did not stop there. He went on to outline the basic processes involved in respiration. Although his presentation only scratched the surface of what these students will be learning much later in their study of biology, Walt's introduction was sufficient for their immediate needs and clearly demonstrated the importance of exercising in an area free from air pollution. Walt addressed the class and said, "The air that we breathe has things in it that are good for us or do not hurt us such as oxygen and nitrogen gas. It can also contain things that can harm us." At this point, Walt facilitated a well-organized class discussion on air pollution. Issues discussed ranged from the basic definitions, to ideas on how to measure pollutants, to thoughts on what reduces visibility and/or produces odor (Foster, W. M., & Costa, D. L., 2005). This activity was completed in one class session.

During the next scheduled physical education class, Walt was back in the gym and the students were to participate in an aerobic activity. Prior to class, Walt intentionally wiped the floor with a non-toxic, orange scented cleaner. The place smelled delicious. The observations made by the students were quite interesting. One student asked, "Is the stuff in the air bad for us?" Another said, "If you are in good shape, do you smell the oranges better than someone who is not healthy?" Still another asked, "Once we start running will the smell get stronger since we are taking in more air?" Nothing sounds better to a teacher than relevant questions! Walt quickly put the students' minds at ease by reassuring them that the cleaner he had used is completely safe. They briefly reviewed what they had discussed at their last meeting and then proceeded with the daily activity. Half way through the period, a sweating and panting student said, "I can't stop thinking about what I'm breathing." Walt laughed and told the boy that he had nothing to worry about. The student smiled and went back to his rigorous movement.

Walt turned to me and said, "I hope I didn't scare these kids." We both agreed that teachers should always be mindful of the information their students are, and are not ready for. However, in this particular case, I asked Walt what he thought about the fact that his students are now making cognitive connections and correlations between their bodies and the physical world around them. He responded by saying, "That lesson may turn out to have the most positive impact on my students of any other to this point in my career." I told him, "Because of you, these students may make better choices regarding tobacco and e-cigarettes and be more mindful of their surroundings and the air that they are exposed to." He laughed and said, "Then maybe, we can all breathe a sigh of relief."

Joan always enjoyed covering the topic of pregnancy with her health students. It was something they seemed genuinely interested in. She knew that her lessons had an immediate and positive impact on their lives. However, after attending one of our introductory presentations, she realized there was so much more information that she could be providing. Joan gained an introduction to the field of environmental toxicology and was determined to share her newly acquired knowledge with her students.

Joan has always been an expert on the stages of fetal development. She can tell you when the feet, eyes, central nervous system, heart, etc. develop in the unborn child. This year, Joan added a new and very important component to her teaching, the potential effects of environmental hazards (Kolb, V., 1993). Joan had always explained that outside influences can have adverse effects on pregnancy but now she was prepared to delve into some specifics and found a way to make the information relevant for her students.

Joan made arrangements for a guest presentation from her local Health Department to discuss an employee's "Right to Know" (Emergency Planning and Community Right-to-Know Act EPCRA, 2014). The Health Official explained federal law that provides employee access to information regarding the potential harmful effects associated with chemicals and other hazards in the workplace. Students reviewed actual Material Safety Data Sheets for chemicals that identify the potential hazards for, and precautions to take when working with these particular substances.

Joan decided to steer the dialogue toward what people can and cannot control during pregnancy. The students were given the opportunity to discuss the fact that women who work are forced to make important decisions when it comes to pregnancy. She explained that often, people are not able to simply stop working because they need the income to support their families. The higher-order discussions that followed were truly intriguing. The students discussed workplace safety, parental responsibility, and even tackled the topic of risk analysis. The students concluded that chemical hazards are around us all of the time and we must weigh the risks associated with our decisions and then act accordingly. They added that there is no perfect solution.

Joan explained the workplace is only one of many sources of exposure to environmental hazards that can have adverse effects on pregnancy. She asked the students, "How many of you would like to volunteer to research these potential hazards and report your findings back to the class?" A few students smiled but there were no volunteers. Joan followed up by saying, "How many of you would do the research if you or your wife were pregnant?" Almost all of the students acknowledged that they would. The Health Department Official applauded and said, "That's great. You must always remember that laws may be there to keep us safe but being well-informed is the best way to protect you and your loved ones."

Joan could now move on with her unit on pregnancy. Her students are now aware of environmental hazards. They realize that there are agencies to help keep them safe and there is a wealth of information at their disposal. Most importantly, they will have the opportunity to make informed and intelligent choices that may one day keep them safe and perhaps, protect the lives of their unborn children. How many employees are aware that they have the right to know? Joan made sure that all of her students are!

Pat is the Head Girls' Basketball Coach for her high school, a retired middle school science teacher, and an avid supporter of sustainability education. She used her platform as the varsity basketball coach to provide the students and her athletes a lesson in teamwork and sustainability that they will never forget. In order to do this, she teamed up with Ryan, one of the school's biology teachers. Earlier in the year, Pat asked Ryan if he would allow her to assist in teaching the importance of biodiversity by making a guest appearance in his biology class when he reached that point in his curriculum. Intrigued by the offer, he agreed.

When the time to discuss biodiversity arrived, Pat was introduced as a guest speaker in each of Ryan's biology classes. The students were thrilled to find out that they were going to take a break from biology, or so they thought. Coach Pat began by explaining the basic positions on a basketball team and the corresponding responsibilities. "Although there is a lot of overlap of duties," the coach said, "Each position has its own specific role on the basketball court." She went on to explain, "In order to win games, each player must execute her duties perfectly and interact with the other positions while they are performing their specific jobs on the floor. If everyone does her job, the team plays well. Makes sense, right?"

The class agreed as she began a video of a game in action. She told the class to pay particular attention to the blue team and the score. The blue team was clearly demonstrating perfectly executed offense and defense, and of course, winning the game. After a few minutes, Pat interjected, "Watch what happens now." A foul was called and there was a player substitution. Although it was the same team, something was wrong. The team appeared "broken." One student commented, "The player that came into the game must be terrible." Pat remarked, "Actually, that was one of the team's best players." She went on to explain that although very talented, the substituted player was unfamiliar with the role she was required to fill on the court. She explained that due to the fact that many players had already fouled out of the game, the coach was forced to make the substitution even though she knew the team was not prepared for the change. The class watched as the blue team lost their lead and eventually lost the game.

Pat paused and said, "Okay, so what does this have to do with biology? Before any student was able to offer a response, she and Ryan arranged the class into small groups and had them share their individual ideas and eventually, formulate a "team" response to the question. Each group presented its summary opinion and a class discussion ensued. After some debate, the class concluded that Coach Pat had showed the video to make the analogy between a team unable to function properly after the loss of an important player to the failure of an ecosystem to function properly after the loss of an important species. They further concluded that an ecosystem lacking in biodiversity is analogous to a basketball team lacking a talented and deep bench. They explained that both are examples of compromised systems that become vulnerable to any disturbance as demonstrated by the blue team struggling after the loss of a player.

Wow! That was an impressive example of cross-curricular instruction coupled with immediate application to everyday life. Coach Pat and Ryan worked together to give the students a "real world" experience they will never forget. Pat became a very busy person during the next week or so as she was invited into each of the school's biology classes to give her presentation. The lesson morphed over time as the students continued to explore the connection between a basketball team and ecosystems. Students began pointing out how a healthy biodiversity (abundance and diversity of species) is like having a deep bench on a team with multiple players able to perform well at different positions. One student commented, "Biodiversity is like insurance for an ecosystem just as extra players with diverse skills is like insurance for a basketball team."

It is very easy to see the benefit that the biology teachers received from this effort. However, what about Coach Pat? I asked her what prompted her to do this. She said, "I recently read your book, *Sustainable Education*, and remembered the chapter on biodiversity. I immediately thought of this lesson and wanted my players and students to see how applicable an idea like teamwork is, and how it is an integral concept that we must understand in order to ensure a sustainable future for the planet. I also needed my players to understand the importance of accepting their individual roles in order to ensure the success of the team."

I thanked Coach Pat for her efforts and her insight. I explained that what she had done is exactly what I am asking all teachers to do. Simply infusing sustainability education into the learning environment will create eco-literate future leaders. All it takes is a basic understanding of environmental science, the ability to recognize what we call "infusion points" in everyday lessons, and the desire to relate what the students need to learn in class to real world issues in sustainability.

In a project involving the essentials of proper nutrition, middle school physical education teacher Terrance noticed that a large number of his students had used a "Shiny Red Apple" as the quintessential symbol for healthy foods. Most instructors would have missed the opportunity, but Terrance was right on it, "Infusion point!" Terrance used the end of the class period to spark a debate on what naturally grown apples actually look like. Most students had no idea what he was talking about when he said that apples are usually not shiny, perfectly shaped, or bright red. As the bell rang, he told the students that they would continue this discussion.

I was happy to be present the following day, when a student surprised Terrance with several apples he found growing on a tree in the woods near his house. Pointing to the fruit one student said, "Those aren't apples." Terrance responded, "Yes they are. That's what they normally look like when people don't get involved."

Terrance gave the class a brief presentation on the topic of genetic engineering and the use of pesticides. The eyes on several of the students resembled saucers, as if they were watching a horror film. "How many of you did not know that much of what we eat is developed in this way?" asked Terrance. Nearly every hand went up. Terrance then showed his class two video clips. The first was a brief but informative summary addressing genetically modified organisms (GMOs). It was very factual and steered clear of making judgments. The second discussed the use of chemical pesticides in the United States and the potentially dangerous effects associated with them. Terrance asked the class to use their phones to research any topic related to pesticides or GMOs. He arranged the class into groups of five and had them discuss their findings. Each group was given the task of selecting what they considered the most interesting finding. Eventually, each group shared its "top" choice.

Topics ranged from gigantic vegetables and seedless fruits to ethical and safety concerns. Students were openly discussing their findings and Terrance caught my eye and smiled. We both knew that the students were truly engaged. Self-educated on the topic, Terrance was confident enough to ask the class, "What would you like to know more about?" The class settled on "Angela's Spiders." They were referring to the use of predator insects lured into an area to control the population of unwanted pests. Terrance was able to explain that this is a technique farmers often use in place of using chemical pesticides. He used this opportunity to introduce the concept of Integrated Pest Management or IPM and briefly explained how it works (Albajes, R., 2013).

Before the class was over, Terrance directed the learning back to the curricular goal of nutrition by reminding students of the old saying, "You are what you eat," and asking the students to write down their thoughts on what they had learned and how that may influence them the next time they sit down for a meal. One young lady said, "I never realized how far away we are from the food we eat." Terrance asked, "What do you mean?" The student said, "Well, nature seems to be out there, we are in here, and sometimes we don't even touch." I can't help but wonder, should that student someday become a bioengineer working to solve our country's food security issues; did I just witness the moment at which that journey began?

I distinctly remember Maria because in one of our workshops she displayed a special interest during our presentation on risk analysis and management. She stood out as she led her group in an activity that explored the concept of environmental risk in detail. She shared that she had been teaching her health and physical education students about making good lifestyle choices for years. She loved the topic because she knew she was having a positive impact on the lives of her students. As she and her group examined the myriad of environmental risk factors that people are exposed to every day, she contemplated ways to transfer this information to her students without overwhelming them. As most teachers do on a daily basis, she put her creative skills to the task and found the perfect activity.

Weeks later, students entered her classroom and saw large circles of colored paper either on, or pointing to specific items or areas in the room. She divided the class into small groups and said, "Today, you will be environmental specialists conducting a risk analysis of our classroom." The students seemed perplexed and did not know how to respond. "So," Maria said, "You don't think there is anything in here that can harm you?" She then displayed the definitions for "Hazard" and "Toxic" on her touchscreen. Next to the definition for toxic appeared a ferocious looking, but caged lion. Next to hazard was the same lion, however, the door was open. To see if the students got the point, she displayed an image of a cigarette on the touchscreen, pointed to it, and said, "Is this toxic, a hazard, both, or neither?"

Many hands went up. One boy stated, "The cigarette contains chemicals that are toxic because they can harm us if those chemicals get into our body, but it's not hazardous to me because I will not smoke it." Maria said, "Okay, it seems you get the point but what if you inhale second hand smoke? Even if we act responsibly, there are potential environmental hazards around us all of the time." The students began to physically look about the room. Maria said, "Good, you are now wondering if this room has toxic materials in it, and if so, are they hazardous. That is what we are going to explore today."

She gave the class instructions for the day's activity and set them in motion. The students attempted to identify the sources Maria had labeled with the colored circles and then conducted quick Internet searches to support their ideas. The students were heard discussing the ability of people to isolate these toxic materials or manage the hazards that they might pose. Listening as several students used the terms "Risk Assessment and Risk Management," Maria gained the attention of the class and solicited definitions from her students. After wrestling a bit with risk assessment, she turned their attention to the words assessment and management. It was interesting how the class narrowed their definitions down to the following simple analogies; assessment is to analysis as management is to control (Sholarin, E. A., & Awange, J. L., 2015).

Mind you, Maria only facilitated the dialogue. The students drove the discussion and came to their own conclusion that they were evaluating the chances of something happening and identifying ways to prevent that situation from occurring. This is what some environmental scientists, known as industrial hygienists, do for a living. The activity Maria designed eventually produced information the students would use to perform their rudimentary risk analysis.

As a class, the students identified the toxic materials found in each of the items identified by their teacher. They then provided their conclusions with regard to the risk that these materials posed in their present forms. When the activity was completed, Maria asked, "Does this means that the classroom is unsafe?" A student responded, "No, there is always a risk that something will happen, but in this case, most of the risk has been minimized." "What do you mean by minimized?" asked Maria. He said, "The potential hazards have been eliminated or lowered to acceptable levels." The students had identified some impressive sounding chemicals. Not expecting a response, Maria asked, "How do you know what are acceptable levels?" Before the students were able to formulate their ideas, Maria told them to think about that question for next time.

I stopped a young man on his way out of the classroom and asked him if he had anything to say about today's lesson. He said, "I'm more aware of what is around me now. I never even thought about that before today and

I'm looking forward to tomorrow's class. This stuff is really interesting." Maria certainly met her curricular goals as they pertained to healthy lifestyle choices. However, by infusing a little environmental education she will be able to place a big exclamation point in her lesson plans next to the words "Capable of applying what is learned to real world problem solving."

Greg made the varsity baseball team as a freshman and is a member of the school's STEM (Science, Technology, Engineering, and Mathematics) Program. All STEM students in Greg's school are required to develop and implement primary research in an area of their choosing. Having an obvious interest in sports, Greg decided to examine the environmental factors that influence athletic performance.

Tony is Greg's baseball coach and physical education teacher and agreed to serve as Greg's academic mentor. At one of our introductory workshops, Tony was kind enough to share the details of the dialogue he had with his student regarding their project. Tony explained that the first thing Greg needed to do was to become an expert on environmental factors affecting athletic performance. He told Greg, "In order to become an expert on your topic, you have to do the research." Greg responded, "I thought you were just going to tell me to shine a light in somebody's eyes while they're trying to pitch or something like that." Tony laughed and asked, "Isn't it possible someone has already done that? Why would you want to waste your time trying to figure something out if it has already been done?" Greg smiled and said, "You sound like my science teachers. I can see that you're not going to make this easy on me." Laughing, Tony stated that his high school coach used to say, "Baseball is just simple physics," and emphasized that science and sports go hand in hand. Tony instructed Greg that they would meet again in two weeks. During that time Greg was expected to research everything he could about environmental factors that affect athletic performance.

After two weeks, Greg reported back. "So, what did you find out?" Tony asked. Greg placed a mound of notes on the desk and said, "Everything has already been done!" Tony smiled and said, "No, you will find that not everything has already been done." Tony explained that he was happy to see so much is already known on the topic. He then instructed Greg to narrow his focus and continue asking questions and researching to find the answers until he finally asks a question for which he can find no answer. Tony said, "When that happens you will need to experiment in order to provide yourself, and the world, with the answer." All of a sudden Greg's facial expression changed and he beamed with confidence. Tony shared that this was the moment he knew his student understood the process involved in primary research and took the first step toward true independent thinking.

Tony continued to meet with Greg every two weeks to discuss his student's progress. Nearly an entire year had passed before Greg proclaimed, "Okay, I've got it!" and Tony was able to give Greg the green light to write up his critical essay. At one point this may have seemed a daunting task but Greg realized that all he had to do was compile the research and summarize his findings. Greg is now an expert on his topic and concentrating on the experiments that he is currently conducting to answer his most focused questions. Tony made all of this possible by listening to the needs of his student and providing guidance and the tools Greg needed to enhance his own education.

Tony presented the details of this student interaction at a workshop we conducted for his physical education department. At these sessions, we stress the importance of making the learning relevant to the students. You may be surprised to find out how important the field of environmental science is to young people. Greg may be an exceptionally motivated student but because he had a true interest in his topic, he demonstrated how all students are capable of initiating and driving the learning experience when it has relevance to their lives. We may not be able to dedicate years to a single project; however, we can certainly strive to find that common thread that motivates our students.

When last I spoke to Tony, Greg was beginning his junior year and in the process of statistically analyzing the experimental data he collected. I can hear the pride in Tony's voice when he speaks of the accomplishments of his student and player. I hope you can sense the pride I have in teachers like Tony who provide the opportunity for their students to reach their full potential. According to his supervisor and principal, Tony is an outstanding physical education teacher, however he is much more than that to his students.

As my first department supervisor once told me, "Remember, you are not teaching your subject, you are teaching students." I encourage you to heed those words. In the big picture, today's youth inherently understands what they need to learn in order to succeed. Try to keep an open mind as to what your students truly need as you implement your daily curriculum. You too can make physical education a sustainable education.

Chapter 6 – Righting History

I have always been fascinated with the relationship that exists between environmental science and social studies. You really cannot teach one without, at least, referring to the other. What is truly fascinating is that many social studies teachers already instinctively infuse environmental education into their lessons. In fact, with the exception of the core sciences, I have witnessed more environmental infusion occurring in social studies than in any other discipline. As a practicing sustainability coach, my advice to social studies teachers is to make sure that they identify and document the infusion points of environmental education clearly so that others may follow their lead and opportunities are not missed. The following is a brief "history" of some of the more memorable examples of sustainability education carried out in the social studies classroom.

Terry is one of the most enthusiastic teachers I've ever met. She takes every opportunity to relate her curricular material to the lives of her students. She will tell you, "If it matters to them, it matters!" When it came time for her to explore the ancient Polynesian culture, which once inhabited the mysterious island of Rapa Nui, also called Easter Island, she asked me to stop by. She said, "You'll definitely like this one." She certainly was correct. I loved it and I think you will too.

I must have heard her students saying, "Whoa that's cool!" over ten times as she showed her class pictures of the huge iconic statues or moai built by the early inhabitants of the island. She handed out informational material to her students and asked them to silently read about this once thriving civilization. Historians believed that these people met their demise, presumably due to deforestation and resource depletion. However, recent studies are pointing to invasive species, disease, and slave raids as being the actual culprits. (Jarman, C., Guzmán, A. J., Fernández-Pérez, N. A., Svoboda, E., & Follis, K., 2018). After distributing large poster sheets and markers (this must be a regular activity as the students seemed to know exactly what to do) she asked her students to discuss what they had read, and work collectively to formulate and write down their observations and comments on the Rapa Nui civilization. The class discussion that ensued was jaw dropping.

The first group to volunteer their ideas drew the Earth on one side of their sheet and sketched the island on the other with the mathematical sign for "equals" in between. "I think I already know where you are going with this but please continue," said Terry. She later admitted she had not given her students the credit they deserved, and that they were one step ahead of her. They had carefully read the information they were provided, applied higher-order thinking, ingenious analysis, and made some very astute observations. The students explained that even if the early assumptions regarding Rapa Nui are eventually proven inaccurate, when people first arrived on Easter Island around 300 AD, they probably saw unlimited resources and felt that they could take whatever they wanted from the land forever. The students made an analogy to the way most human beings currently view the resources on our planet.

Recognizing that her students were focusing on the issue of sustainability, Terry interjected and introduced the phrase "Planetary Management." She explained that some people hold the opinion that human beings are the dominant species and have the right to transform the world to suit their own needs. "Well, we think that is what the Rapa Nui people must have thought, and even if resource depletion wasn't the actual cause of their extinction, it certainly serves as an interesting analogy to our society. We feel that if people continue to deplete the Earth's resources, common sense tells us that eventually, everything will be used up," replied the group.

The entire class was now involved in the discussion. Terry said, "The Earth is so big. How could this ever happen to an entire planet?" One student pointed to the picture of the Earth and said, "The Earth is alone in space just like Easter Island is alone in the Pacific Ocean. It's just bigger so it is going to take longer for us to run out of resources." Another student added, "That's true, but the world's population is also increasing and that will speed things up." Terry allowed the other groups to have time to share and discuss their team's ideas with the rest of the class. The students debated the information provided in class as well as additional sources that they had pulled up on their phones. The overall conclusion was that we might never really know what happened to the inhabitants of Easter Island, however the mere possibility of them causing their own destruction by depleting their resources should serve as a "wake up call" for humanity.

In my opinion, this is where Terry did something heroic. It would have been easy to continue this very disheartening discussion. Instead, she introduced the concept of sustainability. She explained that the technology exists to spare us from the once believed fate of the people of Rapa Nui. Pointing to the students, she said, "History is in the past, what happens in the future is up to you!" Terry kept the conversation extremely optimistic and uplifting. She introduced the students to several career opportunities that they could pursue that would have immediate and positive impacts leading to a sustainable society.

Suddenly, I remembered that old phrase that we all have heard time and time again, "If you fail to learn from history you are bound to repeat it." Right in front of my eyes the students were applying what they had just learned to their own lives and that of future generations. They were acquiring the motivation and the tools needed to solve real world problems that their generation will inevitably be facing. When educational leaders strive for college and career readiness in the classroom, this is what they mean.

Participating in Terry's class brought to mind a personal anecdote that I must share with you. After meeting with a sustainability education colleague who teaches at Florida Atlantic University, my wife and I were able to escape to nearby Deerfield Beach for a few hours of relaxation. It happened to be the day that an artificial reef for divers was to be positioned about a mile off the coast. The artificial reef was an artist's breathtaking, concrete recreation of the huge moai statues of Rapa Nui. The structure had been built on a large platform barge and was being positioned by several vessels. Knowing that this was to be a diver's paradise, my wife and I watched intently from the shore. All at once the barge was released, the huge statues flipped as the structures descended and eventually landed upside down on the bottom. My wife and I turned to each other and just blinked. We felt the pain of the artist and the organization that paid for the effort. There is probably some prophetic moral to that story. I'll leave that up to you.

Dylan is a social studies teacher. In one of our introductory workshops, he learned about biological hazards to which we may be exposed on a daily basis. He was especially interested in the policies, procedures, and technologies that protect us, and how often we fail to acknowledge or appreciate their importance in our society. He stated that the next time he discussed the Middle Ages and the plagues that severely impacted civilization, he would also instill some current environmental education into his teaching so that the students would see the relevance to their lives.

As expected, Dylan did an excellent job educating his students on the Bubonic or Black Death plague. He developed group activities that allowed his students to examine the possible causes and impact that the disease had on the European communities. The class learned how society adapted, norms changed, and how cultures eventually recovered from this terrible plague. When the unit was completed, Dylan explained that the students would be assessed in a manner similar to past exams except that this time there would be a second component, involving creativity, ingenuity, and teamwork.

In preparation for the exam, Dylan decided to spend a class period discussing toxicity and specifically, the field of epidemiology. The students seemed intrigued and asked, "Will this be on the test?" Dylan replied, "I won't ask you to repeat any of the definitions but I will expect you to apply what we cover today to what we have been learning about in class." Dylan then summarized the fields of toxicology and epidemiology quite succinctly. He concentrated on biological agents and routes of entry into the body. State of the art control procedures and technologies were examined and discussed.

As promised, the first half of the assessment was exactly what the students had come to expect. One student proudly said to Dylan, "That was easy." Dylan thanked the student for his honesty and said, "You really didn't have to think too much, did you? That is sometimes the problem with most exams as they are too easy for you guys. Tomorrow, you will need to use your knowledge in a creative way. Don't worry about your grades," he added, "When it comes to the second component, you will be graded on effort."

The next day students were observed working in teams to develop scenarios that may have prevented the plagues of the Middle Ages. There were no right or wrong answers, just many young minds working collectively to propose valid solutions to a real-world problem, and hopefully in the process, raise their current assessment scores. Dylan decided to give the students an extra day to complete their projects as the level of engagement surpassed what even he was hoping for.

Most groups were able to hand in their written proposals by mid-period. This allowed Dylan time to relate the activity to what some students may find themselves dealing with as future leaders. He explained that the people of the Middle Ages did not possess our current knowledge of disease, were caught off guard, and were therefore at the mercy of this biological hazard. Dylan looked right at the class and said, "I hate to be the bearer of bad news, but with our ever-increasing population, the threat of another plague is imminent. You, however, have the power to prevent a catastrophe such as this in the future. Based on the activity we just finished, how many of you now feel that you could have helped the people of the Middle Ages?" Every hand went up.

Dylan then asked the class if they considered "preparing adequately for a future plague" to be a priority for the next generation of leaders of our society. One student responded, "There are so many problems that it's hard to prioritize, but yes, if we don't make it a priority, a plague could be as devastating as any of those issues." Dylan said, "Good point, a lot of people are going to get paid large sums of money for addressing those problems. Just curious, are any of you interested in learning more about the fields of toxicology and epidemiology?" The majority of hands went up. Dylan's initial smile morphed into a look of concern, as he clarified by saying, "Doing so would not be in place of regular social studies class!" The students laughed and there was a silent pause in the room. One student raised her hand, saying, "I feel like I want to go back and change the past. Thanks for making us feel like we can change the future." Dylan, laughed and said, "Old people like me are counting on it."

Brendan's students were learning about the industrial revolution. He wanted to make sure they understood the role fossil fuels played during this period of incredible economic growth in our country's history. In order to do this, he applied a concept we discuss in our introductory workshops referred to as "Current vs. Ancient Sunlight" (Hartmann, T., 2004). Brendan told his class that the Native Americans used current sunlight for all of their energy needs whereas the people of the industrial revolution relied on ancient sunlight. The students seemed to be confused by his statement.

Brendan went on to explain that when the sun shines on the Earth, plants absorb the incoming solar radiation and build biomass (grow) using substances found in the soil, water, and air. This biomass is capable of temporarily storing the sun's energy. Before European settlers came to America, the native people used the energy stored in the plants to burn as fuel, feed their livestock, or eat to meet a portion of their nutritional requirements. Used or not, the energy was released sometime in the lifespan of the plant and transferred in some way to the environment and eventually back to space in the form of heat. Brendan summarized by saying that the sun's energy took a one-way path directly through the plants and animals, into the environment, and ultimately escaped to space. He explained all of the energy was used in real time or currently and that is why it is referred to as using "Current Sunlight."

Brendan asked the class, "If what I just explained describes current sunlight, what do you think is meant by the term ancient sunlight?" There were many interesting responses, however, Brendan heard exactly what he was waiting for when one student answered, "Ancient sunlight is solar energy that was once in plants and animals and is now trapped in the ground." Brendan pointed at the student and said, "Bravo! What do we call stored energy?" Another student raised her hand and answered, "Fossil fuels like coal, oil, and natural gas."

The students shared that in their science classes they had learned about how energy from the sun gets stored in the Earth. They explained how plants and animals that lived millions of years ago died and became trapped in the ground. Pressure and time allowed the energy to become stored in the chemical bonds of what we now call fossil fuels. In order to release the incredible amounts of energy available in these fuels, one only needs to break those bonds. In other words, burn the fuel. Brendan added that whereas current sunlight belongs to us, using fossil fuels is like "stealing" sunlight that belongs to the Earth. He said it required millions of years for the Earth to make these fuels and once they are used, they cannot be replaced.

In order to demonstrate the problems associated with a society becoming reliant on fossil fuels, Brendan developed a clever and effective activity. The assignment required that the students perform simple mathematical calculations involving energy input and product output data. Calculations were to be performed over a 300-year time period and for two societies, Native Americans and people living during the height of the industrial revolution. Although several assumptions were necessary in order to keep the calculations simple, the results were certainly reliable enough to make a point.

By the time the students had finished their calculations it was obvious the product output during the industrial revolution dwarfed that of the Native American society. Following a brief discussion, one of the students said, "I guess people just learned how to be more efficient." In response, Brendan said, "That's an interesting idea. Let's perform one more set of calculations and revisit your statement."

In the second set of calculations, both groups of people were again to be compared except that this time the calculations were to use data spanning a 3000-year time period. It only took a few minutes for the class to realize Brendan's point. "Wait," said one student, "This isn't fair because the ancient sunlight is going to run out before the 3000 years are over." "You're right," said Brendan "but go ahead and finish the calculations." A few minutes went by and a young man said, "Even with their resources running out, the people from the industrial revolution still have an overall higher product output so they win." Brendan asked, "Really? Do you win if you run out of something that you rely on for your survival?" The student who had made the comment on efficiency pointed to Brendan and said, "Well, at least we now know how we can make adjustments to become more efficient!"

Brendan asked the class what word best describes how the Native Americans lived with regard to their use of "Current Sunlight." I always enjoy sharing the actual words that the students gave to Brendan for answers: efficient, smart, intelligent, unselfish, prudent, and last but not least, sustainable.

Rob's elementary school students were learning about the early pilgrims that settled in what is now referred to as the New England area. The class studied the reasons for their leaving everything behind in hopes of finding a better life in a far-off land. The students also gained an introduction to, and appreciation for the hardships that these people encountered. One often overlooked or briefly mentioned problem for these early settlers was their failure to grow certain crops that they had successfully cultivated back in their homelands. Rob briefly discussed the causes for this inability and was surprised by the number of students for which these concepts seemed completely unbelievable. Rob, however, was eco-literate enough to adequately address the issue and was confident that he could do so in a manner that would not disrupt his planning for this curricular unit.

Knowing that it would be several years before the topic would be covered in their science classes, Rob decided to show the students a brief video that focused on the importance that each species and every environmental component has on the health of an ecosystem. When the video was finished, Rob asked the class what they thought of the presentation. One boy said that it made a lot of sense but it was "weird." "What do you mean?" said Rob. The student replied, "It's weird that we are talking about science in social studies."

I have learned that what the child was saying applies not only to how some students view the different subject areas but how many teachers and administrators do as well. So many educators continue to teach their disciplines in "silos." This may result in their students' failure to recognize the need for interdisciplinary approaches when solving real world problems. However, what Rob did next demonstrates the ability that one single teacher can have in correcting this deficiency and the overall enormous influence that each of us can have on the educational process and lives of our students.

Rob asked his class to reflect on the video in terms of what they had been discussing. He assembled the students into groups and directed them to develop an explanation for why crops from European ecosystems may not be successfully cultivated in America. What made the assignment so interesting was that the students were to prepare their presentations as if they were actually going to have the opportunity to meet with and speak to the pilgrims before they were to leave on their journey.

The students set right to task and the level of engagement was exceptional. The presentations themselves were equally impressive. Already familiar with the hardships that the pilgrims would be facing, the students explained the need for them, as a species, to integrate into the existing ecosystem. They also warned against disrupting the ecosystem itself as that too might ultimately result in unexpected and unwanted consequences. The students demonstrated a proactive approach to protecting not only the settlers but also the existing, native ecosystem.

Another outstanding characteristic of this project was that Rob found a way to include an environmental component in his lesson by enhancing, not disrupting the existing curriculum. To that end, the students were so engaged in the activity that they not only explained the environmental issues they had just learned about but also loaded their presentations with nearly every area of deficiency that had been discussed in class. It truly seemed that they wanted their pilgrims to succeed.

Rob commented that he appreciated how the students appeared to take ownership of the project. He asked them what they enjoyed about this activity and why they put so much energy into it. Rob shared several of the student responses with our workshop attendees as he thought all might benefit. He started with one student that said, "This project showed us that if we learn from the past, we can use that knowledge to prevent or solve future problems." Another said, "If more teachers did what you let us do today which was to use what we know to prevent problems, maybe the world would be in better shape." His favorite response came from a student who said, "This was cool because we got to do what adults are supposed to do." When I first heard that statement, I didn't know how to feel. Rob reminded us, however that perhaps his students will remember this lesson when they assume leadership positions. He also explained that there are other teachers in his school that are doing what they can to infuse environmental education into their instruction. I think that gave all of us an immediate boost of optimism for the future.

I thanked Rob for sharing his infusion strategy with us and for also doing such a fine job demonstrating how simple the process of enhancing the curriculum in this manner can be. Most importantly, Rob reminded us that every eco-literate teacher has the power to change the world with a little bit of ingenuity. One of our workshop participants added, "If every teacher infused one environmental concept into their lessons just four times each year, imagine what an impact that would have on our children's ability to lead their generation into a sustainable future." If that were the case, our children would certainly not fall for anyone attempting to tell them that climate change is a hoax, that the world is flat, or that the sky is falling.

After covering the end of World War II, Chris and his students had a discussion about nuclear energy. He was astonished to find out how little they knew about the topic. One of his students claimed that he was told nuclear power is the solution to our energy crisis and that all of this talk about renewable energy is a waste of time. That was all Chris needed to hear. He decided to use the remaining fifteen minutes of class to infuse a little bit of much needed environmental education.

Chris pulled up a website that effectively displayed the schematics of a nuclear power plant. He explained that instead of the energy being released all at once as in a military weapon, it is released in a controlled manner so that people can put the energy to productive use. By the looks on the students' faces, one could see that they were truly interested in what he was saying. Chris affirmed that we do get an incredible amount of energy from a nuclear reaction but it also requires a lot of energy and money to obtain it safely. As a result, the overall or "net" energy that we actually get is not as high as, for example, the burning of fossil fuels. "I knew it was too good to be true," said the student who introduced the idea. Chris agreed with the student's comment but added that when it comes to energy, there are options available that are quite good and are "true," they are called "renewable" sources. Chris knew that he piqued some curiosity but decided to save that discussion for another day and turned the students' attention back to nuclear power.

Chris explained that in addition to the low "net" energy recovered there is another problem with relying on nuclear power. He said that the nuclear waste created during the process releases harmful radiation and can remain hazardous for extremely long periods of time (Lee, 2019). "For this reason," Chris added, "we must find a way to safely store, destroy, or somehow render this material harmless." Chris typed out the homework on the touchscreen. The assignment was to research feasible methods of managing nuclear waste. He promised that he would collect the responses so he warned the class to take the assignment seriously.

To begin the following class, Chris collected the homework as promised. He then organized the students into teams and randomly handed back the responses. He gave the students ten minutes to read the potential nuclear waste disposal solutions, discuss their individual ideas, and propose what their team believed to be the best option available while providing supporting evidence for their selection. One by one the groups offered their solutions and effectively supported their conclusions. It was apparent from the discussions that followed each presentation that what may have seemed as the clear choice for one group, was considered a poor choice by another. However, after all of the groups were finished presenting, the class discussion supported a completely different conclusion. The students agreed that there really is not now, and may never be an acceptable solution to the dilemma caused by hazardous nuclear waste.

Chris was visibly pleased with the level of engagement and praised the class for their efforts. A young lady raised her hand and said, "This is so important for people to know. Before yesterday, I had no idea that nuclear waste could emit radiation for tens of thousands of years no matter where or how it is disposed of. It scares me to think people in charge of making important decisions may be equally unaware." Chris responded, "That's why I'm making sure that you know the truth so that someday, when you are in charge, you will all be in a better position than today's leaders and make sensible decisions."

I asked Chris if he had planned to infuse this concept into his instruction. He told me, "Absolutely not and a year ago I would not have even considered it." However, since reading *Sustainable Education* he continues to make a conscious effort to identify infusion points in his teaching. Chris said, "It increases the students' interest and motivation. I've found that it doesn't take long at all and it keeps the students focused on the content for which I am ultimately responsible." He then put his hand on my shoulder and said softly, "Our department supervisor loves to see my students taking such an interest in their own learning so my last few evaluations have been terrific. Don't tell her I said that." Sorry Chris, I just told the world. You are certainly doing your part in developing the eco-literate leaders of tomorrow. Keep up the good work!

While Shana's social studies class was learning about racial injustice and social inequality, she seized a great opportunity to introduce her students to the concept of the NIMBY (Not In My Back Yard) Syndrome (Wright, S. A., 1993). In addition to explaining the economic reasoning that politicians have used to justify their decisions for what many consider environmental inequality, Shana decided to educate her students as to some of the social problems associated with materials production (Teixeira, S., & Zuberi, A., 2016).

Shana began her lesson by asking her students to simply list things that they enjoy having, or would like to have. Responses ranged from houses, cars, and boats to smartphones, computer games, and food products. She arranged the class into groups and directed them to research the unwanted waste and/or pollution associated with the production of their selected items. After discussing their findings, Shana said, "Since we now have an appreciation for the enormity of the problem, perhaps one of you can tell me what the 'Not In My Back Yard' or NIMBY Syndrome means?" One student offered, "It means don't put the bad stuff where I live. Put it somewhere else." Shana asked, "Like where?" The student responded, "Some place where no one will have to deal with it." Hearing that, Shana replied, "Let's see how easy that is to do."

Shana distributed a group activity she had designed to reinforce the social problems associated with materials production and its unwanted byproducts. The activity focused on the production of an imaginary item she called the "Plark." In the activity, Plarks are in great demand and producing them creates many job opportunities. It is an economic benefit for any community willing to allow Plark production in its town. Unfortunately, Plark production releases high concentrations of particulates (smoke) in the immediate vicinity and also produces an unpleasant odor. Although neither of these issues is considered unreasonably toxic, any home near a Plark factory will certainly experience a drastic reduction in property value.

The activity required the students to zone their imaginary town in order to accommodate a Plark factory. Students were provided basic environmental data associated with the byproducts of Plark production. Students were observed aggressively discussing where to place the factory. Arguments in support of the factory concentrated on the financial benefits to the entire community while those in opposition focused in on the environmental degradation as well as the economic losses suffered by those residents living near the plant. One student was heard saying, "Nobody knows for sure that the particulates going into the air are safe. What if someday we found out they cause cancer or some other disease?" One could see that the students were engaging in higher-order discussions.

As the period was about to end, Shana told the class they would have more time tomorrow to finish their zoning. One student raised his hand and said, "Even with more time, there is no way to do this fairly. Someone is going to get stuck with the Plark factory. It only makes sense that we put it where the property values are low." Another student stood up and said emphatically, "That's not fair. You will just make things worse for the people who are already poor!" Shana thanked both students for their comments and said, "That is called social injustice. We will be discussing that in depth tomorrow."

Shana certainly got the attention of her students by making the topic relevant and actively involving them in the process. She was also able to infuse some concepts of environmental science into her instruction. The activity she designed included some basic environmental information that the students needed to understand and consider when making their zoning decisions. As a result, the students are now familiar with ambient air quality, pollution standards, and toxicity.

Witnessing the "buzz" of the students as they exited the room was testament to the incredible job that Shana did as they were all heard talking about what they would be discussing tomorrow. Shana's activity demonstrated highly motivated students, higher-order discussions, and real-world problem solving. Shana used a very simple strategy to infuse environmental education into her teaching. Great job!

◆◆◆

Kyle teaches US History and knows that he is making an impact on the future. He believes that one of the most important goals for today's educators is to develop eco-literate leaders capable of making sound decisions that will ensure a sustainable society for their generation and those that will follow. Kyle works diligently to meet that goal and is an inspiration to his peers and students.

Kyle assigned a project that required his students to research a prominent American figure they felt had a significant impact on the economic growth of our nation. In its present form, this typical assignment would have been enough for him to meet his unit goals. However, Kyle decided to infuse environmental education in order to enhance the learning and motivate his class by making the core content more relevant to the lives of his students.

In addition to providing an explanation and supporting evidence for why the student had chosen a particular individual and describing his/her impact on the economic growth of the Unites States, Kyle asked that they also reflect on the impact that this person's contribution is having with regard to the future sustainability of our planet. Understandably, the student presentations were a bit different than what may have been expected had Kyle not included that last requirement. Almost every report identified at least one way in which economic growth resulted in some type of environmental degradation. Kyle said that during the presentations, it was interesting how the students seemed to focus more on the environmental consequences than the economic growth. When he inquired about his observation, Kyle said one student's comment summed it up best, "Past generations made money at the expense of the planet's resources. That's illogical and selfish since the survival of our species depends on the availability of those resources and the future belongs to us. We can still make money but we need to do it wisely."

Kyle shared the content of several of the presentations with our workshop group. There were two he felt best demonstrated the significance of the assignment. The first student selected Nelson Rockefeller. As most of us would expect, the young lady began her presentation by describing one of the most influential, charismatic, and successful Americans in the history of our nation. The student portrayed Rockefeller as a brilliant entrepreneur that helped build our country into what many consider to be the most powerful in the world. She gave a colorful account of how Rockefeller used ingenious production methods and effective distribution strategies to bring oil to millions of Americans and how he paved the way for this fossil fuel to become one of the backbones supporting the country's infrastructure.

The student's report went on to explain how our country became the superpower that it is today mainly due to the effective exploitation of this natural resource. She maintained that our nation continues to rely on fossil fuels and is now addicted to it. This astute young lady had the courage to infer that we traded away our energy independence and natural resources for the "American Way of Life." The student added that in addition to resource depletion, our dependency on oil has caused enormous environmental degradation in the form of soil, water, and air pollution. She ended her report by asking her peers a very interesting question, "Had Rockefeller never succeeded, and had the United States never become dependent on fossil fuels, would climate change even be an issue today?"

The second student selected Henry Ford. Few will argue that the Ford Motor Company had an enormous influence on developing and providing our society with one of the most useful tools ever conceived, the automobile. This young man began his presentation by acknowledging the points made by the first presenter. He was able to demonstrate that the automobile, although another backbone of our country's great economic success, has contributed significantly to the environmental degradation of our planet. The student presented the class with reliable emissions data and documentation to support his claims. The class appeared to be mesmerized when he recounted a story describing the regret that one of Henry Ford's grandchildren and company successors must have felt. Realizing how far the automobile industry has grown since its inception and how overindulgent our society has become in that regard, the relative had a crisis of conscience as he considered his family's contribution to our world's current environmental condition. At the conclusion of his presentation, he reminded the class of the first student's question and asked them to imagine what the world would be like had fossil fuels never been discovered. He then asked, "Even if they had been discovered, what would the world be like if all automobiles were powered by water, air, or the sun, not fossil fuels?"

After the question was posed, Kyle said the class went silent.

Kyle remarked that he was amazed by his students' ability to connect our world's reduction in natural capital and environmental health with our economic growth. He said that we often underestimate the ability of our students to analyze, use, and extrapolate information to form their own conclusions. Reflecting on this assignment, Kyle said, "Although I considered the project an outstanding learning experience, it did make me uncomfortable because I realized that our way of teaching may be isolating our children from the truth. Perhaps, we need to just lay it on the line for our students and let them make up their own minds." That was one of the most memorable moments for me as a sustainability coach.

While studying "Life on the Plantation," Kathy's gifted and talented class wanted to know why it was a considered a crime for plantation owners to teach slaves how to read or write. Kathy did her best to explain that with knowledge comes power, and the slave owners were threatened by the idea of educated slaves. She said that suppressing education is a way for people in power to maintain their control over others. There were many teaching strategies that she could have used to reinforce this idea but Kathy knew she could take it to the next level. She believed that if she could make the practice of misinforming or withholding knowledge from people for gain relevant to her students, Kathy would provide them with a life skill they would never forget.

Kathy realized that she might be treading on a very sensitive topic so she touched base with her supervisor to make sure that she was not imposing her own political views on her students or disrespecting those of others. After seeing what she was planning her supervisor said, "This is an outstanding idea, and what education is all about. I do see your concern, however, if you remain completely factual you are simply proving your point that knowledge is power. You have my full support." Armed with the backing of her administration, Kathy confidently moved forward with her lesson plan.

Kathy told her class, "It may seem like we are getting off topic but we are not." She asked, "How many of you smoke cigarettes?" Not one hand went up. "Why not?" She asked. One student replied, "Everyone knows it's bad for you. Smoking causes cancer." Kathy said, "That's great that you are aware of that fact. Many people my age were not. Had we been made aware of the hazards associated with smoking, several of my friends who died of lung cancer might still be alive." Kathy then summarized the history of our country's tobacco industry. She described the intentionally misleading advertisement campaigns and economic reasoning behind the deception. She explained the programs that many industry leaders and politicians implemented whereby scientific evidence was suppressed or manipulated for economic gain. The students seemed horrified as if this could never happen in America. Kathy explained that it was only through years of legal struggle and relentless efforts of consumer advocacy groups that cigarette packages now require the warning labels that they do (Willemsen, M. C., 2018). Kathy asked, "Are you starting to see why education is so important? The more you know, the more difficult it is for you to be deceived."

At this point, Kathy had the undivided attention of every student. She then gave a brief but accurate description of climate change. She went on to explain that not everyone accepts that climate change is real and if you research the topic, you will find that some people claim that it is an elaborate hoax. When she was done, a student asked her, "Do you accept that climate change is real?" Kathy smiled and said, "It doesn't matter what I think. What matters is what you think, because if it is real, you are the ones who will have to live with the consequences."

Kathy provided the class with access to the Internet and asked them to find out all that they could on the topic of climate change. She allowed the students to work in groups, adding that if there were unresolvable differences in opinion, students were free to join another team that held a similar viewpoint to their own. Kathy directed her students to keep an "open mind" and required that all statements made in their presentations must be supported with credible, scientific evidence. The students were given the entire period and the first 15 minutes of the next to complete the research and develop their presentations.

Kathy asked all of the groups that accept climate change to move to the right side of the room and those that did not to move to the left. Laughter rose from the room as every student moved to the right. "Does anyone have the courage to state that they do not accept climate change?" asked Kathy. There was no response and then a moment of silence as Kathy visually scanned the room. "All of the reliable scientific evidence supports that climate change is real and is happening," said one student. By the visual nods and verbal acknowledgements of the students, the statement was obviously well received by the rest of the class.

"So that's it then," said Kathy. "Since climate change is real, all we have to do is get down to solving the problem, right?" One young man raised his hand and said, "That's the way it should be but not everyone does their own research and many people believe the misleading or false information that they are being told by others who have something to gain by telling lies." Kathy was amazed by the simplistic clarity of the student's statement. She said, "You know, some people will argue that one person's truth is another person's falsehood. What do you have to say about that?" One brazen student said, "I found and can provide two documented statements made by important governmental officials that are clearly lies meant to mislead people." Kathy asked, "In defense of those individuals, is it possible that they are simply misinformed themselves? Oh," Kathy added quickly, "and please don't mention their names or their titles." The student said, "Then they have no business serving in their positions if they are not intelligent enough to understand an issue like climate change. Also, knowing what these people have to gain by using deception and denying the scientific data, I am too intelligent to accept that they are simply uninformed themselves."

Kathy sensed that she was now treading on the sensitive topic that she had discussed with her supervisor. Confident she had made her point that knowledge was indeed power and that suppressing education is a means by which people in power continue their control over the less informed, she turned the discussion back to life on the plantation. Kathy asked, "Does everyone now see why the plantation owners were threatened by the thought of a well-educated slave population?" The comments from this gifted and talented group were quite interesting, and Kathy did ask me to share her favorite. Her student said, "It is our education and our ability to make up our own minds that keeps us free. If we chose to ignore science and fail to challenge what we are told then perhaps, we are gambling with our freedom."

Jacob's US History class was studying the labor unions of the early 1900s. One of these groups, the United Mine Workers, seemed to resonate with a particular student.   It turned out that several of the student's relatives happened to be in the mining industry.   She shared that a few had died from "Black Lung Disease." Recognizing that her peers were genuinely interested in hearing more about her relative's experiences, Jacob asked the student if she would be willing to share her family history as it related to class. After she agreed, Jacob said that when she was ready, he would give her time to present her information. Although a worthy effort, Jacob sensed that it was a sensitive topic for the student. He told her that she should not feel obligated to follow through with his request.   "Oh no," she replied emphatically, "People need to know about how difficult and dangerous coal mining really is. I want to do it!" Jacob ended up getting much more than he bargained for.

When Jacob reached the unit in his instruction where he planned to deliver information on the hazards associated with coal mining, he identified it as the appropriate infusion point for some environmental education. Having discussed the presentation with the student ahead of time, Jacob knew this was the perfect opportunity for her to initiate and drive the learning process. The young lady began her report with a very comprehensive account of the history of coal mining in the United States. She explained that coal was considered the primary source of energy from the 1800s until the 1950s and how it continues to play an important role in meeting the country's power needs. Hearing her speak, one could tell that she really knew her stuff. She provided the class with positive economic data and balanced that with anecdotes of mining disasters and worker hardships. Jacob had shared with our workshop attendees the fact that he could not have covered this material any better himself. However, what the student was uniquely able to do so effectively was demonstrate the relevance to her classmates.

Having completed the factual history and practices associated with mining, the student focused everyone's attention on the personal lives of her family members who had either died or were impacted by the hazards associated with the mining industry. She showed several pictures to the class. Some of them were old, black and white photos while others were more recent. She said that she didn't want the class to feel sorry for these people but rather hoped that they would understand what happens when people are ignorant of environmental hazards. She showed a very short video describing human respiration. The clip explained how oxygen needed by the body is transferred to the blood and exchanged for carbon dioxide in the lungs. The student then continued with a second video that used an animated model to demonstrate how particulates can interfere with the process of oxygen exchange. She described pneumoconiosis or Black Lung Disease. (Schroedl, C. J., Go, L. H., & Cohen, R. A., 2016). The class listened intently as she delved into the epidemiological aspects of the disease. The student's ability to effortlessly relate the scientific information while she was providing a qualitative description of the effect that the disease has had on the personal lives of her family was remarkable. Jacob said that she sounded more like a first-year doctor in residency than a high school student.

When she completed her presentation, her classmates applauded and then inundated her with a myriad of questions. Jacob helped facilitate a class discussion focusing on air quality and its effect on human health. Having participated in one of our introductory presentations on sustainable education, Jacob was comfortable explaining the basics of air pollution to his class. He exposed them to the country's fundamental air quality regulations and standards.

For some students, this was the first time that they realized how important yet vulnerable our air actually is. One student said, "I heard that our government wants to increase coal production and is willing to sacrifice our air quality. I've seen pictures of people in China wearing masks. Is this going to happen to us?" Jacob certainly enjoyed the higher-order discussion and was unwilling to curb the high level of engagement but knew that he had to guide the discussion and keep it grounded in the facts. "No," he said, "as you and your fellow students become aware of the environmental consequences associated with increasing fossil fuel consumption and loosening regulations on the associated emissions, I am confident that future leaders will chose a better route that transitions to renewable energy."

Jacob was pleased to see that the discussions remained factual and that politically motivated rhetoric never played a role in the lesson. He directed the students' attention to the homework assignment and thanked his volunteer for her outstanding presentation. The class again applauded her as the bell rang.

One of our workshop attendees asked Jacob if he was ever nervous that the student would say or do anything incorrect or inappropriate. Jacob said that since he was familiar with the subject matter, he knew he would be able to steer the instruction as a facilitator if needed. He said that it was refreshing to witness the students driving the learning process and how well they seemed to assimilate the information and initiate relevant discussions. I asked Jacob if the training that he received from SEA had helped him in this effort. I loved his response. He said, "I remember you telling us that a consultant is like someone who borrows your watch, tells you what time it is, and then hands it back along with a bill. In this case, I decided to read my own watch. Thank you." For those of you who have never been to one of our seminars, I think he meant that we gave him the direction and confidence to make himself eco-literate and he was able to take it from there. Well, I hope that is what he meant!

I'll never forget meeting Lindsey for the first time. One of our presenters was organizing an activity in which teachers were required to brainstorm infusion possibilities for their curricula. Before we even began our break out session Lindsey blurted out, "I know exactly what I'm doing!" The group laughed and looked at her. She said with confidence, "Sorry, I just thought of something that will be perfect."

At the workshop she and her team developed an outline for a very interesting project that would require the students to compare the Roman civilization to our own in terms of its sustainability. After the analysis and comparison, the students would be expected to create a scenario in which our society would not "fall" as did the Romans. At the time, we were all impressed with the group's potential activity. What was more impressive was when Lindsey actually pulled it off in her classroom. A few months after our seminar, Lindsey gave us a call and invited us to her school to observe the implementation of a version of the lesson that had been originally developed at the workshop. We were thrilled at the opportunity.

Lindsey's class had obviously been studying the ancient Roman civilization as evidenced by the recent projects displayed throughout the classroom. Knowing her individual students' strengths and weaknesses, she organized them into teams and provided each with specific responsibilities. Lindsey had obviously spent much time developing this project as she had already identified the three areas of sustainability (economic, environmental, and social) that each group was to be responsible for researching and analyzing (Learn About Sustainability, 2016). The ultimate goal was the creation of a sustainable scenario in which, unlike the Roman civilization, our society does not fall victim to its own way of life.

Lindsey provided the class with a brief but comprehensive overview of sustainability. As an example of a society that was not sustainable, she recounted the story of the Mayan civilization and demonstrated the economic, environmental, and social issues that contributed to its demise (Fattouh, T. N. 2017). She showed the class pictures of actual Mayan ruins that she had taken on a recent trip. It was clear that Lindsey's enthusiasm was infectious as her students pried her for more information. One student said, "It's so sad that people who could have built such amazing cities would allow themselves to be destroyed by their own actions." Lindsey responded, "Yes, it is, however, were they really able to prevent it? Could the Romans have prevented their fall? Most importantly, can we prevent ours?"

Over the course of several days, Lindsey provided her students with what she called "guide posts" that served to keep the students on task, meeting immediate or short-term goals, and moving toward their ultimate project deliverable. The students were given access to all of the resources available in the school's media center and quiet areas that allowed them to discuss their findings. Students were observed setting up charts and diagrams that assisted them in comparing and contrasting our society to that of the Roman civilization in regard to the three areas of sustainability. Many higher-order discussions were heard within and between the different student groups. Eventually, the teams developed visual aids and prepared the dialogue for their presentations.

Lindsey's project was so well planned that every team's presentation effectively compared our current society to that of the Roman civilization in each category. Some groups compared the two qualitatively while others chose to do so in a more mathematical and quantitative manner. The class consensus, however, was that direct comparisons were not simple. The teams concluded that the civilizations were so different one could only make the observation that each civilization, in its own way, is unsustainable. "Wow," said Lindsey, "are we in that much trouble?" One student raised his hand and said, "No. If we start making changes now, we can certainly avoid what happened to the Roman civilization." Another student added, "We have the advantage of technology. We are now a global civilization and if we all work together, we have the ability to live sustainably. We just have to use our technology in an intelligent manner."

Already a success, Lindsey looked to "hit the homerun" by adding a final component to the project. Giving her students one additional class period, she directed them to create what she called their, "Ten Sustainability Commandments" for our society. She explained that they were to imagine that they had the power to develop "Ten Directives" that nations would have to follow in order for our world to become truly sustainable. She added that these "Commandments" must be realistic and feasible, however, that doesn't mean they have to be easy to comply with or accomplished without sacrifice.

As expected, the students came through again. Each team presented their "Commandments." After each presentation, interesting discussions ensued that gave all of us a sense of true optimism. These students were planning out a guideline for a future of sustainability. Little, if anything, they were proposing was impossible, and just seeing those potential future leaders in action, without anyone else's influence was enough to make us all believe that there is hope for the future of this planet.

Lindsey certainly went above and beyond the call of duty when it comes to infusing environmental education into her instruction. She dedicated much time and effort to this project. This is something that we at Sustainable Education Associates do not necessarily advocate on a daily basis. However, when I asked Lindsey the basic question, "Was it worth it?" she replied, "Think about it. Once I set everything up, how hard was my job? Yes, I would definitely do it again." She had a term for what she was doing. She called it, "Righting History."

Chapter 7 – The Right Chemistry

I did not start out as a science teacher. Instead, I began my professional career as a public and private sector environmental scientist and served for several years as an instructor for the Rutgers Department of Environmental Science. With such a solid foundation in applied chemistry under my belt, one would think that when I did shift gears and entered public education, I'd feel right at home. Boy, was I in for a surprise.

Although I was very comfortable in the classroom, I was used to putting my chemistry background to practical use and problem solving, not presenting material directly out of a textbook. I soon realized that the other teachers simply introduced students to the very basic fundamentals of chemistry and followed a rigid curriculum with pre-established laboratory activities. I felt extremely awkward and out of place. It had been over ten years since I actually studied basic chemistry. I knew the only way that I was going to survive was to rely on what I had learned in the field and do all I could to incorporate that into my lessons. I thought, "Perhaps, no one will find out that I'm faking it. I'll just do this until I figure everything out."

Well, it didn't take long for the other teachers to see that I wasn't following the usual system. They kept trying to get me to use their lessons and standard labs but the truth was I did not see the value in much of what they were doing. I specifically recall one activity in which the students were instructed to burn a candle and list their observations as either physical or chemical changes. I remember thinking to myself, "You have to be kidding. No wonder these kids don't appreciate chemistry." Not wanting to make waves, I had the students follow the lab procedures but I also required them to assess the potential impacts that these physical and chemical changes might have on the environment. I could tell that the other chemistry teachers were not too happy with me. How dare I mess with the sacred, instructional methodology that had been employed for decades? A few days later my supervisor asked to see me in his office. "Oh boy," I thought as I entered the room.

"I love what you're doing," said my supervisor. "This is exactly what I had hoped for when we hired you." I really meant it when I asked, "What do you mean?" He went on to say, "You're bringing the real world into the classroom. I knew you had the background and hoped you might be willing to share that with the students." I said, "The truth is I'm not as proficient in chemistry as the other teachers, I have to rely on applying it to what I had been doing as an environmental scientist." My supervisor laughed and said, "That's funny, you don't even realize what you are doing! You are making the students use the basics to evaluate situations and apply what they know to solve problems. You are already doing what only the best teachers do. I am hoping that you will help your colleagues and our department to improve in this area."

That meeting was a turning point for me. I will always be thankful for how well my supervisor handled my integration into the school and nurtured my relationships with my peers. Through the years, he was quietly supportive of all that I was doing and never forced the other teachers to alter their instruction. Infusing environmental education into my lessons came naturally to me but that was only because I enjoyed the advantage of a background in environmental science. I must admit, however, that I was eventually humbled by many of my colleagues that had not started with such an advantage, yet had at least become my equals when it came to promoting eco-literacy in the classroom. My supervisor certainly knew what he was doing.

Nearly twenty years later, when I was offered and accepted the position, I had the privilege of following in the footsteps of that great man. As Science Supervisor, I too was able to appreciate and understand the validity of assisting teachers to bring the relevance of their subject matter into the learning environment by requiring their students to apply acquired skills in real-world problem-solving scenarios.

Today, when school leaders contact Sustainable Education Associates, they sometimes refer us to their science supervisors and this is unfortunate. Actually, I am hoping that anyone who is reading this collection of educational success stories realizes that eco-literacy in the classroom is every teacher's responsibility. I will, however, concede that it is the science teachers' responsibility to lead by example. There is no longer any excuse for a science instructor to avoid infusing environmental education into their curriculum. Everyone is looking to them for leadership in sustainability education.

In general, you may notice that many of the representative accounts provided for science are more detailed than those for the other disciplines. That is no coincidence as most science teachers have an advantage when it comes to sustainability. In many progressive school districts, science teachers are already expected to infuse environmental education into their instruction. In fact, for the vast majority of science teachers, it is already a part of their curricula. For those of you who are striving to promote sustainability in every aspect of your scientific learning environment, thank you and keep up the good work. However, for those of you whose schools are not yet on board, it is time to talk to your leadership and get your district moving toward a sustainable future!

Kim has been instrumental in developing the ongoing relationship that exists between SEA and her school district. She has been infusing environmental education into her lessons for years, however, after reading the book *Sustainable Education* given to her by a colleague, she knew that with a little bit of outside assistance she could help her school become a leader in sustainability education. One day, Kim's principal was giving us a tour of their school. While in the science wing, we happened to be walking past Kim's classroom. The students were moving between classes at the time and she was standing by her door. Kim asked us if we wanted to see sustainable education in action. How could we refuse?

Kim began her class by reviewing a unit that chemists refer to as "Types of Chemical Reactions." She used an animated video that described and provided examples for when; two or more chemicals combine to form a new one; a substance breaks up to form two or more new chemicals; an element replaces another from an existing compound forming a new material; chemicals recombine to result in different substances; and a particular reaction that involves converting a fuel and oxygen into carbon dioxide and water (Kotz, J. C., & Treichel, P. M., 2018).

Before any of us had the chance to lose concentration, she initiated an automated slide show along with soft music and the sound of rain. A few photos into the presentation she said, "During the next few minutes, please see if you can make a connection between what we have been learning in class and the images that you are seeing on the board." The images were of outdoor items such as statues, car roofs, buildings, etc. that seemed to be worn or "pitted."

When the slideshow was finished, Kim asked, "Okay, so how does this apply to types of chemical reactions?" One student raised his hand and said, "All of the things that you showed us were getting worn away by the rain." "Can you be more specific?" asked Kim. "The water must be reacting with elements in these materials." replied the student. "Great job!" said Kim, "Does anyone know the term that scientists use to describe this process?" Several students called out, "Acid Rain." "Good, you've heard of it," said Kim, "Now, we are going to look at acid rain or acid deposition through the eyes of a chemist."

Kim distributed a lab activity that she designed specifically for teaching the chemical processes behind acid rain and its detrimental effects on the environment (Images, D. W., 2017). "Tomorrow," she said, "we will be conducting a wet chemistry lab that will demonstrate how substances called acids are created when primary pollutants in the air react with, and become dissolved in water. We will also see how those acids, considered secondary pollutants, later undergo a single replacement reaction with outdoor materials." Kim instructed the class to read the handout for homework. She then said, "It's imperative that you understand the importance of this topic and how it can affect all of our lives so please pay attention to what I'm about to show you, and yes, it will be on the test!" Kim used the remainder of the class period to show a video describing how acid rain is formed. It also identified the detrimental effects that acid deposition can have on both living and non-living systems.

I could not wait to come back for the lab activity and it was well worth it. As Kim's students entered the room, they donned their safety gear, proceeded to the lab stations, and awaited further instruction. "Before we begin," Kim asked, "how do you feel about today's lab?" A student raised her hand and said, "It's going to be interesting to actually perform the chemistry that goes on in the air that we breathe." Had I not known Kim's reputation for incredibly relevant activities, I might have thought she put the student up to her answer. The student continued, "You show us why we need to learn chemistry." That was one of the best compliments that I ever heard a teacher receive from a student.

Kim's lab did not disappoint. The activity reviewed the basic chemistry involved in two of the five types of chemical reactions that the students were learning about. First, they mimicked the reaction that takes place when water comes in contact with air pollutants in the presence of sunlight to create acid. They also performed a single replacement reaction in which the acid alters the composition of a substance resulting in changes to its chemical and physical properties.

As the students organized their data and began the cleanup Kim said, "When you write up this lab report, please spend a little extra time on your conclusion. Be sure to support why our goals and objectives were or were not met." I noticed in the "Objectives" section of the activity that the goals were to "reinforce and experiment with two examples of chemical reactions and to be able to explain the formation of, and potential detrimental effects of acid rain." I can tell you from experience that Kim's students were certainly provided every opportunity to meet those goals.

Looking critically at this lesson, one can see that by infusing environmental education into the activity, Kim was able to enhance the learning without disrupting the existing instructional strategy. Kim is an expert in this area. She is a recent college graduate whose professors methodically train their education students in eco-literacy. She is a product of an educational program that values the infusion of environmental issues not only in science, but all disciplines.

Top universities and colleges have been practicing sustainability education for years and producing eco-literate graduates such as Kim. However, we must remember that not all high school graduates go on to study at the college level. For many people, high school may be the highest form of education that they will receive. In order for our society to become truly eco-literate, sustainability education, like that provided by Kim and all of the teachers you are reading about in this book, must be integrated into every educator's instructional strategy.

Jim teaches all levels of chemistry and is always looking for ways to improve the learning experience for his students. This veteran teacher will be the first to admit that he does not enjoy lecturing. In addressing our workshop participants, he said, "Sometimes while I am lecturing to my students I start boring myself to sleep." He explained that when he was less experienced, he did a lot more talking, and his students did a lot less learning. He said whenever possible, he creates a scenario in which the students can teach themselves while he serves only to facilitate the activity and provide guidance when needed. One workshop participant said, "That sounds a lot easier than it probably is." Jim replied, "The truth is that if the activity is well designed and you know your content, facilitating the process is actually quite easy."

Jim agreed to share an example of something he had done recently. Jim explained that he finds the topic of "Expressions of Concentration" to be one of the most difficult concepts for his students to master (Ways of Expressing Concentration, 2018). He told us that when he first started teaching, he would usually define the basic terminology, demonstrate the standard problem-solving techniques, assign practice scenarios, and eventually conduct an appropriate lab activity. Jim said, "When I look back on that, I cringe. In order to get the students to take initiative on their projects, I first try to motivate them by establishing relevance."

In an attempt to jumpstart this particular project, Jim showed his class a brief clip of winter roads being salted followed by another demonstrating the effects that elevated salt concentration in soils can have on vegetation. After a brief discussion, he posed a simple question to his students, "What concentration of calcium chloride (rock salt) in runoff water should be used to effectively melt snow and ice but avoid adverse effects on the local environment?" Talk about a loaded question!

Jim knew that classroom management was extremely important for the success of this project. Groups were assigned based on student skills. Laptop computers provided ready access to the Internet. Jim anticipated the student needs and made appropriate equipment and materials available in the classroom. Jim commented, "Whenever I run inquiry-based activities like this one, it pays to think ahead as to what the students may need or request. It avoids you having to run around and search for items."

Jim provided his class with activity guidelines that outlined the methodology they were expected to follow to develop and conduct an experiment designed to provide sufficient data that would allow them to propose an appropriate concentration. The guidelines also made it clear that the students were given free rein to use whatever equipment and supplies were available in the lab. If students felt that they needed any outside materials, they were to submit a simple request form. If possible, Jim would get the item(s) for them.

Jim established time allotments for the students to conduct their research, experiment, discuss, analyze, or do whatever was needed to eventually answer the original question. Students were provided approximately one half of each class session during a two-week time period to complete their work. The guidelines also identified the presentation requirements, as each group would be expected to state their final conclusion and support their findings using their experimental and researched data.

Jim told the workshop participants that one of the hardest things to do while facilitating a long-term project such as this is distinguishing between the questions that the teacher should answer and those best left for the students to figure out on their own. Jim provided us with the following example. A student asked him, "Should the concentration be expressed in percent, molarity, or molality?" Jim suggested that this was an example of a question best answered by the students. By simply saying, "You tell me," Jim explained that you might initiate a higher-order discussion involving the different expressions of concentration. Jim said, "It is during these discussions that the true learning takes place. I have heard students defining terms and discussing the advantages and disadvantages of using the different expressions. Why should I stand up there and lecture when students are more than capable of uncovering the information, wrestling with applications, and forming their own conclusions? You do, however, need to know when to step in and guide the dialogue. At a certain point, the students may turn to you for your experienced opinion. If you feel that they have exhausted their resources, this is totally appropriate."

The students spent a total of three weeks working on their project while according to Jim he was able to continue making progress toward his standard curricular goals. Students were observed discussing procedural issues, devising bioassay experiments, collecting and analyzing data on the growth of seeds cultivated in various concentrations of calcium chloride, and forming conclusions. The process was quite impressive.

Jim explained that the species of plant seeds, chosen in order to be representative of the flora for the area, were not uniform among the groups. Nor did all teams express their concentrations in the same manner. Some used percent concentration whereas others used molarity or molality. "That was the beauty of the activity," said Jim, "Instead of presenting my understanding of expressions of concentration to the students and them repeating it all back, the class was able to research the topic on their own, internalize the issues, and eventually, the students were able to come to their own conclusions."

I had the privilege of observing the concluding session for that activity. As the groups presented and supported their final conclusions, the entire class discussed and debated the findings. Arguments were heard in support and in opposition to many issues. Jim facilitated the discussion by organizing the ideas into categories and summarizing the class conclusions on the touch screen. When all was said and done, the board resembled professional class notes on the topic of expressions of concentration. Jim printed out hard copies of the summary and distributed them to the students. Jim advised his class, "Tomorrow we will review expressions of concentration. Your assessment will be the following day. Please take some time tonight to review the material and prepare any questions that you may still have on the topic." I asked Jim if I could see a copy of the exam. It was a typical assessment for this concept in chemistry. "How do you think they will do?" I asked. Jim said, "Funny you should ask. I was hoping to share the results with you anyway."

I explained to our workshop participants that several days after the exam, I was able to review the results. They were outstanding. "See," Jim said, "If the students are motivated, they initiate and drive their own learning. All you have to do is set everything up and watch." I reiterated to the group that teachers do not have to go to the lengths that Jim did in order to promote eco-literacy. Oftentimes they can simply discuss a topic, make a quick reference, or explain a point of relevance. Jim agreed but added, "In time, you may find that it's worth it to find ways to integrate environmental education that provides your students a reason for why they are learning a topic. It is the relevance to a student's life that motivates and drives the learning environment forward."

Jayda is one of the college prep chemistry teachers for her high school. She needed to cover single replacement chemical reactions and told me that while she was scanning through the chemical storage room for appropriate reactants, she remembered our Sustainable Education presentation. She thought, "Why not expose the students to the mining industry and the potential environmental impacts that it poses?" Armed with the fundamental concepts that she had learned in our seminar, she selected sulfuric acid and chunks of chrysocolla, a natural copper ore.

Before conducting the lab, Jayda wanted to set the motivational stage. She was determined to demonstrate how the mining industry affects our planet and how much this topic actually relates to her students and their world. Although she already possessed a fundamental background of the process, Jayda brushed up on the topic so that she was confident enough to present a comprehensive and accurate overview for her students. So much for giving the students the opportunity to ask, "Why are we learning this?"

Jayda began her lesson with an introduction to the different types of mining techniques. She defined the term "ore" and explained how the valuable mineral found within it must be extracted using physical, or in most cases, chemical means. The students were visibly interested as they were already asking intelligent questions. Jayda then pulled up a schematic that outlined a smelting process used for extracting iron. She said the lab activity that the class would perform is similar in nature to this process. "Just one more thing," Jayda added, "I found something that I think we all should watch." Jayda pulled up a brief documentary that summarized the environmental degradation that mining can cause. The video focused on the soil, air, and water pollution aspects. When the video ended, Jayda said, "Although we don't have any more time to dedicate to the practice of mining right now, if you are still interested, we will find time to revisit the topic in a future class."

Jayda distributed the laboratory handout and reviewed it with her students. "Today we are going to take a piece of copper ore called chrysocolla and follow the process that the mining industry uses to extract the usable copper metal from the residual waste materials called gangue." Jayda summarized the lab procedure explaining that the students would crush the rock to increase the surface area and then add concentrated sulfuric acid to the pulverized ore. The acid would undergo a chemical reaction with substances in the rock to produce a blue green solution called aqueous copper sulfate. The waste products would be physically removed by passing the solution through a filter, and then, introducing a piece of iron metal (iron nail) into the system. The iron replaces the copper in a single replacement reaction. Jayda said, "In this reaction, we say that the iron leaches into the solution producing iron sulfate and the copper comes out of solution as a precipitate or solid." Jayda emphasized the importance of safety as she reiterated that the students would be working with concentrated sulfuric acid and that the byproducts are also hazardous.

As I circulated around the room, it was impressive to hear the students discussing the chemistry involved in the lab. However, it was equally refreshing to hear their dialogues concerning the mining process itself. "Wow," I thought, "this is a chemistry class and these kids are making connections well beyond the walls of this room!"

Jayda had obviously struck a chord with her students. Strictly from a chemistry standpoint, they performed admirably during the lab activity. However, in wrapping up, Jayda asked the students to write and submit an "exit ticket" describing what they learned and what they would like to know more about. Jayda shared the reflections with me. Both of us were amazed that nearly every student's response with regard to what they had learned focused on the relevance of the activity to the mining industry. Similarly, almost all wanted to know more about the potential environmental hazards.

Jayda wanted to make good on her promise to revisit the topic of mining and we were pleased to share our experience with her class. Since one of our Associates had professional experience with that particular type of hazardous waste handling, we immediately set up a guest presentation for her class to address the subject in detail. The students certainly showed great potential as future environmental scientists. I have to say that her students' enthusiasm spilled over onto our presenters. Jayda was also glad to have us in the day before winter break because as she put it, "They're not going to listen to me today anyway!"

On a serious note, Jayda's effort proved to be an outstanding example of infusing environmental education into the instruction. She was able to cover all of her curricular requirements without sacrificing any of her content. As any of these eco-literate teachers that you are reading about will attest, by demonstrating the relevance of what the students are learning, you will drastically improve the motivation and level of engagement. This can only enhance the learning environment, increase student comprehension, and improve problem-solving skills. Jayda, everyone digs your lessons. Sorry, I just had to say it!

Prior to entering public education as a chemistry teacher, Ted had once worked as a safety specialist for a municipal health department. Although he enjoyed that position, he had always longed to teach chemistry. He was thrilled to enter the educational profession and thought that he had left his health and safety career behind him. However, as the saying goes, "You can never escape your past." Being that he had a wealth of experience in public employee occupational safety and health (PEOSH), Ted's principal asked him if he would be willing to organize and maintain his science department's chemical storage room. He actually enjoyed volunteering for the job. He found it rewarding to use his experience to keep his fellow colleagues safe and his school in regulatory compliance. As the years went by, Ted morphed into a highly respected educator, beloved by his students.

I met Ted at one of our seminars. A few months later, he called to tell me that he just had a great idea for infusing environmental education into his teaching. After hearing what he was proposing, I asked if I could be part of the process as I too, have a background in health and safety. Ted explained that he was racking his brain for a good way to introduce chemical reactivity to his students. The unit basically deals with what reacts with what, and why. As he walked into the chemical storage room, the proverbial light bulb went on in his head. He said, "They put me in charge of this project because I know what reacts with what, and why. Perhaps, we can develop a lab activity that will help the students understand how a chemical store room is organized and maintained." I replied, "Great idea, let's do it. Hey, if we succeed, maybe they will hire one of the students to take over for you!"

Both Ted and I had served as Right to Know Instructors. In that capacity, we were responsible for informing employees about the chemicals they may be exposed to on the job, the potential hazards associated with those substances, and the proper handling and storage of those materials. Since public employees have the right to know exactly what chemicals they are working with, assisting them to read and interpret Material Safety Data Sheets (MSDS) and Hazardous Substance Fact Sheets (HSFS) was part of the training. Ted and I brainstormed and eventually decided on an activity that would train the students as if they were employees of the school. Ted deserves all of the credit for the development and implementation of the lab as he took it from there.

When the students arrived in class ready for lab, Ted addressed them as company employees. The students realized that something was different and got right into "character." Ted said, "Today you are all employees of the school and you will be receiving your Right to Know training." Ted still had a copy of one of the old videos that he used to show explaining the legal rights that employees have and the basic provisions in the Public Employee Occupation Safety and Health (PEOSH) Act. Seeing Ted in action certainly brought back memories. I enjoyed watching the students' faces as they read some of the potential hazards associated with chemicals that were in their own building. "We have this stuff in our school?" asked one student. "We have a lot more than that but try to remember there is risk in everything we do in life. The idea is to mitigate and manage that risk as effectively as possible," Ted explained. He added, "As you continue to study chemistry, you should be mindful that it must be done in a safe manner. In the chemistry classroom, I have always provided you with safety instructions, have I not?" The students acknowledged in the affirmative. "What about in the real world? Who is responsible for the safety instructions when you someday find yourself in a working environment that may expose you to potentially harmful substances? You are!" Ted said emphatically.

Ted provided the class with cards that represented different chemicals. The students were observed organizing the cards by reactivity in a mock chemical storage room and discussing how the actual substances may be best arranged in a well-ventilated area. Ted advised the class that they would have another lab period to complete this activity. He then conducted a tour of the actual chemical storeroom with the class. "You did this yourself? This would take me years," said one student. Ted responded, "It did take me years. First, I needed to master chemical reactivity. That took some time. Once I understood that, the rest was easy." Ted assured the students that they need not worry. He was not going to mix everything up and require they reorganize the storage room. He said, "What you really need to concentrate on is chemical reactivity. Getting that concept under your belt is like buying a helpful tool that you will have for the rest of your life."

With that one statement, Ted provided all of the relevance his students would need to motivate them for producing outstanding lab reports. In addition to the usual write-up, students were required to interview an individual that works with, or may be exposed to potentially harmful substances on the job and determine the person's awareness of their right to know. Most students interviewed a relative or close family friend.

At the conclusion of the project, I thanked Ted for allowing me to be a part of the process. He returned the thanks and said that he might have overlooked this opportunity had he not been reminded of the importance of infusing environmental education as a tool for demonstrating relevance and sparking motivation. After the activity, Ted received several phone calls from parents, thrilled that their sons and daughters were making connections between what they were learning in chemistry and the "real world." One parent told Ted that he was a practicing chemist and said, "I wish my chemistry teacher had done for me what you are doing for my son. It would have taken me a lot less time to realize how powerful knowledge can be." I hope that all of you may someday receive a call as powerful as that.

Megan had just covered the kinetic molecular theory with her class. The theory states that as temperature increases, molecular motion speeds up causing changes in the physical properties of a system. Megan had already addressed the related mathematical laws with her students and for all intents and purposes, had met the curriculum requirements for the unit. However, recognizing that they are exposed to so many influential leaders that fail to comprehend basic scientific concepts, Megan wanted her students to connect the relevance of what they were learning in chemistry class to the real world. In order to do this, she created an activity designed to demonstrate how an understanding of the kinetic molecular theory is necessary in order to predict the potential environmental effects associated with global climate change.

Megan organized the class into four groups, each given a particular task. Megan said, "After each team completes its individual assigned task, we will attempt to formulate one unified conclusion based on our findings." Group one was given the task of researching and presenting National Oceanographic and Aerospace Administration (NOAA) ice core data on global temperatures for the past 10,000 years. Group two was required to describe and explain the effects that global temperature changes have on the rate of Artic ice melting and the magnitude of annual fresh water release. Group three was required to research ocean salinity data and explain the process by which increases in fresh water affect those numbers. The last group was given the task of researching ocean current circulation patterns and the factors that drive them. Teams were allotted one full class period in the media center to complete their assigned tasks (US Department of Commerce, & National Oceanic and Atmospheric Administration, 2018).

Observing this lesson was an incredibly rewarding experience as the level of engagement was through the roof. At first, students were observed delegating individual responsibilities in order to ensure that their deliverables could be effectively completed on time. Approximately fifteen minutes into the class period some unexpected "crossover" occurred between teams as students from one group began conversing with others. This continued until eventually, there no longer appeared to be four distinct groups but rather one large unit collectively working to achieve a unified goal. "Were you expecting this?" I said to Megan. "No, but this is pretty amazing, don't you agree? I'm not going to stop it," she replied. Both Megan and I realized that something terrific was happening. The students were taking the initiative and the learning was going to happen whether an instructor was present or not.

Listening to the conversations, one could ascertain that students were already piecing together the information that they were individually charged with obtaining. Some looks of surprise could be seen on the students' faces as they shared their findings and discussed outcome scenarios. With a few minutes left in the initial period Megan said, "Remember that tomorrow each group must present their findings in regard to their own assigned task so that together we can make sense of what we have found out." As students left the media center they were already talking about tomorrow's discussion. One student was heard saying, "It's like that movie where the climate shifts and they go into an ice age." Another was heard saying that he was going to do additional research tonight as he couldn't believe some of the data, he had discovered today in regard to Arctic ice melt.

The next day was as remarkable as the first. The students entered Megan's classroom already offering what they had found to their teacher. Megan was visibly pleased with their enthusiasm but asked them to wait until everyone was ready to discuss their findings. Megan began by posting the class objective on the touchscreen. It read, "Today we will share our findings and demonstrate how an understanding of the kinetic molecular theory is necessary in order to predict the potential environmental effects associated with global climate change."

In turn, the groups began to present their findings. The first group reported that all of the scientific data that they were able to find suggests that the overall temperature of the Earth is increasing and doing so at a faster rate than at any time in the past 10,000 years. They added that most scientists are in agreement that human activity is to blame for this phenomenon. The second group reported that the increase in global temperatures has resulted in an abnormally high degree of Arctic ice melt. In fact, they said climate scientists are now realizing that their predictions need to be revised as they have clearly underestimated the effect that global warming would have on our polar ice caps to date. Group three reviewed the concept of concentration and provided the class with data supporting the fact that ocean salinity values are decreasing in certain areas due to the incredible amounts of ice melt. They explained that this occurrence is responsible for altering the density of the affected water as well. Finally, group four presented a brief report on ocean circulation patterns. They explained how these currents, or oceanic conveyer belts determine the fundamental climates and corresponding ecological biomes around the world. They went on to define the driving forces behind these ocean circulation patterns. They emphasized that differences in water densities that rely on ocean salinity values is one of the major factors driving oceanic currents.

Although I have done my best to summarize what the students had reported, I have not done them the justice they deserve. The class discussion that followed these presentations was similar to watching a skilled artist sculpt a masterpiece out of a lump of clay. Right before our eyes, Megan and I observed as the students led their own dialogue, arrived at a conclusion, and supported it with the facts that they had researched. Megan had challenged the students to collectively write one concise statement that addressed what they had learned in this activity and how it relates to their studies. The class selected one young man to facilitate the statement development and display it on the touchscreen. It did not take very long and I was impressed with the students' offering. It read:

In class we have been learning about the kinetic molecular theory. This theory states that as the energy or heat of a system increases so does the speed of the molecules. By heating up our atmosphere, predominantly through the burning of fossil fuels, humans have increased the kinetic energy of the molecules in the polar ice caps. As we learned in chemistry, increasing the speed of solid substances causes them to melt or change phase into a liquid. As a result, the polar ice has been melting at an unnatural rate dumping billions of gallons of freshwater into the ocean. This dilutes the surrounding water and lowers the concentration of salt in the ocean resulting in a decreased density of the solution. The major oceanic conveyer belts or currents move in specific patterns based on the existing salinity concentrations and water densities. Eventually, it is very possible that these patterns will shift with the drastic changes in density. The biomes that exist on our planet have developed over tens of thousands of years based on the existing ocean currents. Adjustments in these currents could result in immediate climate shifts. Life on our planet is not prepared for such an unnatural event.

During my last few years as a public-school administrator, we were required to perform quantitative evaluations for our teachers in the classroom. There were many scoring strategies, and our district employed one that rated different categories of a teacher's lesson. Megan created a learning environment in which all of the curriculum content was introduced, reinforced, and applied. Students were immersed in high-order discussions and observed working collectively to problem solve and create a plausible cause and effect scenario for a real-world issue while applying the concepts learned in the classroom. This lesson would go down as "distinguished" across the board!

As do all good teachers, Steve constantly thinks about his students and how to improve their learning environment. One day he had a great idea for infusing environmental science into his instruction and how he thought of it makes for an interesting story. Steve explained that he and his wife were anticipating the arrival of their first child. In preparation for the momentous occasion, Steve was painting the former guest bedroom sky blue per his wife's instructions. After only a few minutes of the activity, he felt dizzy and was experiencing a headache. Steve realized that he should have known better and went to the store to buy a respirator. When he arrived, he was surprised by the wide variety of options that were available on the market. As he started reading the labels, he realized that addressing the basic principles involved in respirators would serve as an excellent application for the topic of physical versus chemical separation.

Steve began his class presentation wearing a canister-type, air-purifying respirator. The "wow" factor was quite effective as the students listened intently. Steve mumbled as he addressed the students, "Today we are going to discuss an application of what we have been learning about in class, mainly the concept of chemical versus physical separation." Steve removed the respirator, pointed to it, and said clearly, "That's better. How many of you know what this is?" "It's a gas mask," replied one student. "You're kind of right, but actually, it's an air purifying, canister-type respirator specifically designed to remove volatile organic compounds. Say that ten times fast!" Steve challenged.

Steve explained that there are two main types of respirators; supplied air systems and those that purify the air before it is inhaled into the lungs. Supplied air systems pump in fresh air and are needed in extreme situations. Air purifying units, on the other hand, remove impurities from the ambient air making it safe for breathing. Air purifying units separate the harmful substances from the air stream by employing either a physical or chemical process. Steve said to think of an air-purifying respirator as a device that either uses a fancy filter (physical) or chemical reaction (chemical) to get the job done.

Steve began by describing a HEPA (High- Efficiency Particulate Air) Filter. This air-purifying device prevents small particles like pollen, smoke, soot, sawdust, and even mists from entering the lungs. He explained that this and other "filter-type" respirators operate using physical separation techniques. In other words, no chemical change occurs. Pollutants are simply separated from the air. These devices range in price depending on the porosity or weave of the fabric.

Steve then described cartridge-type, air-purifying respirators that employ pollutant-specific canisters that remove toxic gases and vapors from the air that we breathe. These involve chemical separation techniques. The chemical reactants in the cartridges are specific for the type of toxins in the gas or vapor stream. Examples of these pollutants include formaldehyde, acid gases, and volatile organic compounds. Many of the cartridges use activated carbon or resins that adsorb or chemically alter the pollutant. These can be tricky to use and much more expensive because they only work until "saturation" or the chemical reactions have reached completion. Saturation rates depend on concentration and other factors like breathing rate and humidity levels. Special training is required to properly use these respirators (CDC -

Respirators - NIOSH Workplace Safety and Health Topic, 2019).

After his presentation, Steve asked the students to think about how important it is that people understand these concepts. He explained that using the wrong respirator for a particular substance or wearing it improperly can result in serious harm or death. Steve then described the role of an industrial hygienist to his class. He said, "An industrial hygienist is someone who gets paid to make sure that people are safe in their working environments. These professionals must understand the basic scientific principles involved in air purifying techniques since they are responsible for selecting the proper respirators. Their duties also include ensuring that employees know how to use the respirators, and that they fit properly."

"How do they make sure that a respirator fits," asked one student. "They perform a qualitative fit test," said Steve. He continued, "They ask the employee to put the mask on and then they spray a non-toxic substance that has a distinct odor around the mask. If the employee is able to detect the odor, the mask does not fit properly." "That doesn't sound very scientific," said the student. Steve responded, "Not everything has to be complicated and technical in order to be effective. For example, if you place a substance in water and it sinks, that is a good indicator that it doesn't float." The students laughed and nodded in agreement.

Steve fielded numerous questions from his students including inquiries about people in other countries that need to wear particle masks outdoors, how

SCUBA works, and what happens if a person gets sick or dies from inhaling a harmful chemical on the job. One student said that his father works in an auto body shop and paints cars. He wanted to be able to discuss with him the type of respirator he should be wearing. Steve did an admirable job handling these questions. If he did not know an answer, he encouraged the students to do some research on their own.

After a few minutes, Steve redirected the class back to the fundamentals of chemical and physical separation and reviewed the basics with them. He was pleased to see that the students were not only able to describe these techniques but also capable of applying the various air purifying systems to demonstrate the difference between physical and chemical separation. He then said, "I hope that you all will benefit from our discussion today. I know that I learned a lot just preparing for this lesson." One student raised his hand and said, "This is the most that I have ever learned in a class." "Really?" said Steve, "It sounds like you're just trying to score some extra points!" Another student added, "If all teachers did this, I think more kids would like science." That was quite a statement coming from a high school sophomore. When class was over, I asked her if she would ever consider becoming a scientist. She replied, "I can't believe you just asked me that. During today's lesson, I was wondering about becoming an industrial hygienist." Interesting, in the span of little more than nine months, Steve was able to bring a new child into this world, in the span of a little under 50 minutes he might have also brought us a new scientist. Congratulations Steve, on both counts!

◆◆◆

After participating in our seminar that focused on infusing the concepts of water and wastewater treatment into the chemistry curriculum, Austin envisioned a whole new way of tackling his honors chemistry unit on water, solutions, and solubility by infusing a series of sustainability-oriented lessons. He began his unit with a clever introductory activity that asked the students to imagine that they were all-powerful beings capable of creating their own planet. He said that they would have the power to design their planet exactly how they wished it to be, however they must abide by all of the basic scientific principles of the universe.

"Just one little thing," Austin added, "Before you begin to describe all of the fun stuff, you must first identify how you will address the following three issues or problems in order that your planet and the life that is on it continues to exist." "Man, I knew there was going to be some sort of catch," proclaimed one student from the back of the room. "There always is," replied Austin, "You must: 1) identify how your planet will get the energy needed for sustaining life and the other dynamic processes that may exist; 2) ensure that the moving systems such as materials flow will occur; and 3) determine how your world will cleanse itself." Austin was obviously attempting to introduce his students to the principles of sustainability and also one of the most invaluable characteristics of water, its unique dissolving capability. Confident that his students were already familiar with these concepts, he allowed the class approximately 15 minutes to address these issues.

"Let's start with the first problem. Where will you get the energy for all of your planet's needs?" asked Austin. The students proposed some very interesting and ingenious solutions. Eventually, however, they came to the conclusion that our Earth has the best one-way energy source that the universe has to offer, that being the sun. The students seemed to have a bit more trouble understanding the second problem so Austin rephrased the question by asking, "How do you make sure that materials can cycle, move around, and not just go flying off the planet?" Immediately, the students' hands all went up and they identified the need for nutrients to recycle with gravity playing an important role in this process. Finally, as to how to best cleanse the planet, rain seemed to be the prevailing response.

"So," asked Austin, "Would you say that whomever, or whatever designed the sustainability systems of our planet did a pretty good job?" One student laughed and said, "I know what you did. You just made us say that the Earth is special because it has everything we need to keep going." "Well said! You now understand what is meant by the principles of sustainability," Austin proudly exclaimed. (Miller, G. T., & Spoolman, S., 2015). Austin told the students that he would love to discuss these principles in depth but since they were about to cover the topic of solutions in chemistry, he wanted them to concentrate solely on the third problem, how to best cleanse their planet as it relates to the solubility of substances in water.

Austin explained that chemists refer to water as the "Universal Solvent," because it dissolves more than any other single substance that we know of. Austin said, "In the next few days, you will understand why water is such an effective solvent, how it is purified, and how this all contributes to a sustainable system. You should also be able to explain why and how water's unique ability to dissolve so many substances creates problems for our society in the form of water pollution." Austin then set the students to task on their "Planetary Creations." Austin's students spent the remainder of the period having a blast as they designed their planets. Making sure, of course, that they were completely sustainable.

Austin's next lesson focused on the concept of polarity. He explained that since water is a polar molecule it is able to dissolve other substances that share this chemical characteristic. Since the majority of substances have polarity, the class was able to understand why water is such an effective "solvent" capable of dissolving these "solutes" or substances. Austin distributed the lab handout for the next day's activity and instructed the class to read it for homework. "We will continue with the concepts of solubility and sustainability tomorrow," Austin informed the class.

The next day students prepared for their lab and got right to task. They were examining the effect that temperature has on the ability of water to dissolve a substance. As the students were working, they were heard discussing the ideas presented in the preceding lessons. Although their focus was certainly on the task at hand, they were making conscious connections to the concepts of sustainability. One student said, "The energy from the burner is like the sun. It's affecting the solubility." Another made the connection between differences in density caused by heating and how gravity was playing a part in the mixing of the molecules in the system. Still another commented that the water cycle was one of those "dynamic systems" we were talking about that "cleans" the dirty water.

Would these conversations have taken place had Austin not planted the seeds in his previous lessons? Probably not but more importantly, I had performed this type of lab many times in the past and unlike what had transpired in my classes, one could see that the students here were taking a special interest in their work. Austin had obviously made the learning relevant to them and it was making a difference.

Being a veteran chemistry instructor, Austin had very little problem meeting his curricular goals with regard to teaching the students how to develop and interpret "solubility curves" and the effect that temperature has on solutions. However, what was so impressive about this lab activity and his introductory lessons was the infusion of the environmental concepts. One student told Austin, "While we were conducting this lab I couldn't stop thinking about what we had talked about yesterday." Austin said, "That's good. It means you are realizing why you are learning chemistry."

Austin used a final class period to go over the lab and revisit the principles of sustainability that he had discussed with his students. "Yesterday," Austin said, "You observed how temperature affects solubility. I heard some of you already saying it, but can anyone tell me where the heat or energy needed to raise the temperature of your lab system originally came from?" A young man raised his hand and responded, "We were burning methane gas but that is a fossil fuel that contains energy that originally came from the sun." "Perfect," said Austin. "Now let's think about solutions themselves. If water dissolves so many things, how does it get purified?" Another young man answered, "Water cycles through the environment and when it evaporates, it leaves behind any impurities that it contained. So, in a way, polluted water gets cleaned by a cycling process driven by energy in combination with the law of gravity." "Wow," said Austin, "What does gravity have to do with it?" The student responded, "The water had enough energy to change its density relative to the surrounding air and was forced upward against the pull of gravity and evaporate." Austin put his hands on his hips and said, "Just so you know, I'm not sharing my salary with you."

Austin then used the final minutes of the class period to restate the original curricular goal of the lesson. This was to understand the effect of temperature on solubility. He allowed the students an opportunity to demonstrate what they had learned. He then reviewed what scientists refer to as the three principles of sustainability. Again, the class demonstrated a working knowledge of the concept. "Great job, but we are far from done with sustainability." Austin said, "Tomorrow we are going to discuss some of water's other unique characteristics. I will tell you that water is the only substance whose solid phase is less dense than its liquid phase. For homework, please try to find out why that characteristic is so important when we consider life on our planet."

In speaking to Austin after his series of lessons, I asked him if he could keep this up. He showed me the "Planets" that the students had designed in the opening lesson. These imagined worlds were the most symbolic evidence of our children's ability to create a sustainable future that I had ever seen. He said, "I used to teach chemistry, I obviously do much more than that now. You know, the enthusiasm that these kids are showing is contagious. Their level of engagement and concern for their world is inspiring." That is quite a concept, students inspiring teachers motivating students. Now, that is what I call a sustainable education!

During their unit on electrochemistry, Aaron had recently introduced the topic of fuel cells and the students were conducting a corresponding lab. He was confident that he had covered his curricular goal since his students were able to quantitatively demonstrate the relationship between the chemical changes that were occurring and the corresponding electricity. Out of the blue one of Aaron's students began asking him questions about solar cells. Aaron briefly explained the basics of how a solar cell works. Another student asked if what they were doing was similar to how the Tesla battery works. Before he could respond, the student's lab partner said, "The Tesla Powerwall uses solar power to charge itself and is able to store the energy." "Wouldn't it be cool if all that we used were solar powered batteries?" blurted out the student at the adjacent lab table (Everything You Need To Know About The Tesla Powerwall, 2019).

Aaron realized that the basic curricular topic of electrochemistry must have triggered some curiosity with regard to green technology and renewable energy. Seeing that the students were motivated to learn more, Aaron jumped on the opportunity and said, "I can see that many of you are curious about alternative forms of energy. It's very important that you learn what they are and the role that chemistry plays. Tomorrow, we will shift gears and take a look at what people are calling green energy. Don't forget that your reports for this lab are due next Thursday."

Knowing that we love to see sustainability education in action, Aaron invited us to take part in the class. He began the next day's presentation by acknowledging Carol, one of our Associates for providing much of the information and activity materials that the students were about to use. Aaron arranged the class into six groups and distributed information on six renewable energy sources, one to each team (What is Renewable Energy? Sources of Renewable Energy, 2019). The students were responsible for reviewing and discussing the information on their particular energy source and then using the prepared visual aid that they were given to provide a brief presentation to the class.

The first group to present was responsible for solar energy. Their visual aid displayed a man installing roof solar panels on a building. Below this image appeared a list of terms and corresponding photos. The students summarized that solar power is energy from the sun that is harnessed and put to use for practical purposes. They provided the class with the basic details of the listed technologies currently being used and improved to provide us with reliable solar energy. The students identified and briefly described solar heating, photovoltaic cells, solar thermal energy, solar architecture, power plants, and artificial photosynthesis.

The next group explained that uneven heating of the Earth causes the air to move and this phenomenon results in wind. Energy carried by the air can be harnessed using wind turbines. Their visual aid was that of a wind turbine along with the basic schematics of an electrical generator. The students identified the blades that are capable of spinning magnets around wires and generating electricity. The students went on to describe wind farms and made a good case for why they can be a viable alternative to the burning of fossil fuels. They stressed the fact that we will never run out of wind and that it is found almost everywhere. They added that there are also no greenhouse gas emissions.

Group three began their presentation by having a student place an eraser on top of a shelf. He said that he used energy to put it there but now gravity will allow that energy to be released as long as we let it fall. They explained that before the eraser drops it has "potential" or stored energy and that when it falls due to gravity it demonstrates "kinetic" or moving energy. The students then displayed their slide of a hydroelectric dam and explained how the moving water is very similar to the falling eraser. However, unlike the eraser, the water is constantly moving and this mechanical kinetic energy can be used to generate electricity. They added that harnessing hydropower is not a new concept and reminded the class of the old-fashioned waterwheels that were once used to power saw mills in our country's early history. The students did point out that, unlike solar or wind power, hydropower is only practical where moving water is present.

The fourth group stood in front of a slide depicting a geothermal reservoir alongside a schematic of a geothermal power plant. "Geothermal energy is heat from the Earth. It can be harnessed to create steam capable of turning turbines and generating electricity," said one of the team members. The group summarized the process involved in making the energy available for practical use. They added that this green technology is clean and sustainable, but limited based on its geographical availability.

The fifth group displayed a picture of a bus and the caption read, "I run on living things!" The students started their presentation by explaining that it's not as simple as putting plants and animals into the tank but the fuel that the bus runs on is produced using biomass. The group explained that the bus uses a biofuel or fuel that relies on biological processes such as agriculture and anaerobic digestion. They said that biofuels are produced by converting the energy found in living systems such as agricultural waste into convenient energy-containing compounds. Pointing to the bus, one of the students said, "This bus requires what is called biodiesel. Biodiesel is produced from oils and fats." The students said that although biofuel is renewable, its production competes economically with other useful products such as our food supplies and is therefore widely debated as a viable alternative fuel.

The final group opened with a clever demonstration. They asked everyone to stand up and slowly walk to one side of the room. When we were all at the wall, they asked us to walk to the other side. Of course, when we got there we were instructed to walk back. Finally, Aaron said, "I think we get your point." The group asked the class, "If you kept doing this you would eventually get tired, right?" The class acknowledged in the affirmative. "That means you are expending energy. The moon's gravity pulls water on our planet back and forth and this energy can be harnessed using tidal electricity generation power plants as shown in the slide." The group stated that the tides are more predictable than wind and even solar power, and therefore have great potential near coastlines.

When all of the presentations were finished, Aaron praised the students for their efforts and again thanked Carol for providing the activity materials. Carol said, "It was so energizing to hear all of you discussing green technologies of the future. There are many career opportunities just waiting for you in these fields. It all starts, however, with the basic fundamentals that you learn in school. Hopefully, all of your teachers will relate what you are learning in class to environmental topics like your instructor has done for you today. A sustainable future will depend on eco-literate leaders. Please keep up the great work."

Aaron told me that he would have liked to discuss these technologies and the application to chemistry in greater detail, however, there just isn't enough time. "You did your part," I said to him. "You certainly have your curriculum to cover. If other teachers do even a small fraction of what you have done here, we will certainly be developing eco-literate graduates. You really are showing that you have the right chemistry!"

Chapter 8 – It's All Simple Physics

Some say that physics is the mathematical and logical description of our universe. If this is true, then physics should explain everything that we see and experience in our lifetimes. It is the quintessential science. This is why the physics teacher plays such a crucial role in the educational development of a student. However, I have heard countless students describe their experience in physics as nothing more than a lot of mathematical equations and they often say, "Since we are never going to use it, what is the point of learning physics in the first place?" If you agree with the sentiment expressed by these students then, quite frankly, your physics teacher might have benefited from taking one of our seminars.

A sustainable society depends on the laws of physics. Like mathematics, there are undeniable and irrefutable rules that need to be followed in our universe. For example, gravity pulls massive objects together, one type of energy always transforms into another of less quality, and for every action there exists an equal but opposite reaction. Nature requires that the laws of physics be followed without exception, yet somehow, the human species has found ways to temporarily "side-step" a few of them in order to immediately satisfy its greed, and for the time being, postpone the consequence of breaking those laws. It is becoming increasingly obvious, however, that our clever attempts to avoid the inevitable consequences of our failure to follow the rules are coming back to haunt us. Well, maybe not us, but they will certainly haunt our children. Never fear, the eco-literate, physics teachers are here!

Nancy's supervisor had been stressing the need for her staff to challenge their classes by requiring the students to productively apply what they are learning in their courses. She asked the teachers to find ways to motivate their students and improve real-world problem-solving skills. Nancy and a few of her colleagues had recently attended one of our workshops. After learning about the various methods of air pollution control strategies, Nancy had brainstormed several ideas with her peers and found that she was almost immediately able to comply with her supervisor's directive.

Her students watched as Nancy held a string that was attached to a rubber ball. Holding on tight, she began to swing the ball in circles above her head. She had several other setups ready and invited her students to carefully imitate her motions and make observations. "In what direction does the ball pull, inward or outward?" Nancy asked. All the students agreed that the force was apparently pulling outward, away from the center. "The outward force that you are feeling from the ball and through the string is referred to as centrifugal force. The force that you are applying to the string to keep the ball from flying away is called centripetal force." She then asked, "If you let go of the string, in what direction do you think that the ball will fly?" "In a tangent to the circle?" a student responded. "Let's test that hypothesis," Nancy said.

Nancy provided the students with a lab activity that gave them the opportunity to investigate both centrifugal and centripetal forces. Eventually, Nancy's class was able to conclude that objects that are exposed to a centrifugal force tend to move to the outside, away from the center. If they are released from the force, they move off in a straight line that is tangent to the original circular motion. Nancy was confident that she had met her curricular goal but not necessarily the one that her supervisor had challenged her with. She still wanted to help her students improve their thinking skills and came up with just the right plan.

Nancy said, "You've learned quite a bit in physics class so far. In fact, if I gave you an exam today, I would bet that all of you would perform well. However, I am going to ask you to challenge yourself in a different way. Today, you are going to show me that you are capable of applying what you have learned to the real world." Nancy arranged the class into three groups, handed out an information packet that described the fundamentals of air pollution and said, "Please take a few minutes to read over this material. When you are done, we will discuss what you have read." When it appeared that the students had completed their reading, Nancy provided a brief review of the material. She specifically concentrated on smoke, dusts, mists, fumes, and vapors; referred to collectively as airborne particulates.

Nancy provided each of the groups with the schematics for one of three different types of air pollution control devices: a cyclone separator, an electrostatic precipitator, or a bag house (Nevers, N. D., 2017). She directed the students, "Now that you have been introduced to air pollution and you certainly understand the concepts that we have been studying in physics class, apply that knowledge and try to figure out exactly how unwanted particulates are removed from air using your device."

Nancy wanted her students to assimilate the information and develop solutions on their own so she did not allow them to perform any research via the Internet. She did, however, permit the students to use their notes, text, and brains, and encouraged them to discuss their ideas and work together to arrive at a conclusion. Several minutes into the group activity, Nancy noted, "You may be realizing that some of the concepts that will apply have already been covered earlier in the year and others we have not yet addressed." "If we haven't covered them, how can we know how to use them?" asked one student. Nancy reassured, "You can use what you do know and apply a little imagination and ingenuity. Trust me. You can do it." Nancy circulated through the room for several minutes. She facilitated the activity but was careful not to influence the problem-solving process. She especially avoided the question, "Is this right?" Instead, she smiled and answered, "We'll see in a little while."

"Okay," Nancy said, "Let's see what you came up with." The group that was assigned the cyclone separator eagerly volunteered to go first. Nancy posted a presentation slide of their schematic on the touchscreen for the students to reference. They started by saying the concept is quite simple and that we had just gone over the physical principles involved. The group concluded that the cyclone separator must work by swirling air in a circular manner similar to what was demonstrated in class using the ball and string. In this case, they identified the particulates to be like the balls. They predicted that the pollutant particles would hit the walls and then move off into tubes and be separated from the basic airflow. "Good thinking," said Nancy, "Without getting too technical, I would just add that this method can also be used to separate droplets of liquid from a gaseous stream as well. Also, larger particles often hit the wall and are removed by gravity." Nancy went on to explain that they could really go into depth by examining Bernoulli's equation and wet scrubbers, but that discussion will need to wait for another time. Nancy praised the students and said they had done a great job putting all the clues together.

Nancy smiled and said, "Let's hear from the electrostatic precipitator team." She displayed the schematic and one student took the lead. "Well, we assumed that this device got its name from the fact that it must work using static electricity." "That's a good start," said Nancy. The student pointed to the arrows indicating airflow and said, "Although we don't know exactly how, here is where we think the air pollution particles become charged. You can see they have a negative charge from the picture and that they move past these large positive plates. We think the opposite charges attract and the particles get stuck to the plates." Nancy nodded in proud fashion. The students ended by saying, "If the airflow is stopped and the charge is removed from the plates, we think the particles will just fall down from the plates and can be removed." "That's basically the strategy," said Nancy. "The particles received their charge by moving through a high voltage created by the device. By the way, you can buy these air purifiers for your home at any department store."

Nancy put up the schematic for the bag house and said, "Okay, where are my bag house people?" The students said that the bag house must work on the basic concept of airflow caused by differences in pressure. One student said, "We think this is basically a big vacuum cleaner but instead of moving the device to the dirt, the polluted air is pulled or pushed using differences in pressure through these big bags. The bags act like filters and the particles must get stuck on them. Just like a vacuum cleaner, we suspect when you turn it off and shake out the bags, you remove the dirt." "That's pretty good," said Nancy. "I would only add that like a vacuum cleaner, the efficiency increases as the particles build up on the filter bags."

Realizing the period was about to end Nancy said, "I wish we had more to time to discuss these and other air pollution control strategies in depth. I do hope that you got something out of this. I know I enjoyed watching you apply what you have learned." One student raised her hand and said, "This was really good because it reminded us why we need to know physics." Another student added, "Yes, and I'll bet that the people who invented these things made a lot of money. All they did was apply some basic physics concepts like the ones we are learning." "Great point," said Nancy, "and what is to say that one of you will not be the next great entrepreneur to come up with some fantastic and better way to clean the air?"

Nancy's supervisor turned to me and said, "Looks like we certainly did the right thing by sending the teachers to your workshop." I thanked her but added the teachers are the ones that need to execute the infusion strategy. By her own admission, Nancy is not an expert in the air pollution control field, nor is she an environmental scientist. She is a teacher and a great one at that. She educated herself as to the necessary environmental concepts and found a clever way to infuse them into the classroom. More importantly, she provided her students with an opportunity to engage in a higher-order thinking activity involving real world problem solving. In parting, I asked Nancy how she learned so much about air pollution since we don't cover all of those control strategies in our seminar. She said, "No you don't, but you did remind us that we all have smartphones." Yep, I did say that!

Jamal is one of those highly energetic teachers that will go the extra mile for his students. They never know what to expect when they come to class. Jamal was true to form the day that he decided to infuse the concept of wastewater treatment into his instruction in order to demonstrate some of the most basic principles of physics that his students had already covered in class. When the students arrived, they knew something was up as the desks were arranged in an odd manner. There was a podium at the front of the room with two long tables on each side. In the middle were seats that resembled those for a "studio audience." "That's right," said Jamal, "It's time to play everyone's favorite game show, Wastewater Wars!" Jamal explained the game rules as well as how credit was to be distributed based on student participation. The rules were designed to engage every student at all times. Jamal showed how the touchscreen technology would complement the competition. Needless to say, Jamal was on his "A" game today.

After the contestant teams were assigned along with their respective studio audience assistants, Jamal began the game by showing a repeating video loop of a bar screen in action. This device looked like a huge set of metal bars with a mechanical rake poised to scrape the attached materials. "This is a bar screen ladies and gentlemen," said Jamal, "A bar screen is the first thing that incoming wastewater or influent goes through. It serves primarily to remove the large solids from the water. The top three answers are on the board. Name a concept in physics that applies to this portion of the treatment process." The buzzer for Team 1 rang, Jamal turned to them as their captain said, "Flow." Jamal said, "Show me flow!" The touchscreen revealed flow as the number one answer. Jamal asked, "Flow is the number one answer, would you like to play or pass?" Okay, I think you can see how the game was to be played.

Jamal continued by showing a picture of a comminutor and said, "This device grinds the larger solids into smaller granules. The top three answers are on the board. Name a reason for including this step in the treatment process." The students responded with "reducing the particle size," and "increasing surface area," but were having trouble with the number one answer.

Jamal agreed with their thought process so far but explained that "'preventing clogging," especially in colder weather was the number one answer. The discussion that followed demonstrated that the students were certainly interested in more than just playing the game and the answers to Jamal's initial questions.

Jamal continued the game by showing a repeating video clip of a primary clarifier. The device resembled a large circular swimming pool with a slowly rotating arm moving about the top. Clear water flowed over the edges. "This is a primary clarifier or settling tank. Its purpose is to remove small solid particulates," said Jamal, "Top three answers are on the board. Name a principle or law of physics that is at work as the particles settle to the bottom of the tank." What was truly impressive was not that the students were able to guess all three of the answers Jamal had listed, but that they were able to put up a good argument for why the relationship of Q = AV or flow equals area times velocity is more applicable than gravity. Never the less, the game continued.

Up on the screen appeared a video clip of what looked like a huge rectangular swimming pool the size of a high school gymnasium. The brownish water was in constant motion as huge bubblers were pumping air into the water. Looking up at the screen Jamal said, "Here we have an aeration tank. The major purpose for this step is the breakdown of organic wastes. The top three answers are on the board. Name a scientific discipline, other than physics, that will be at work in this step." After the number one response of "biology" was provided, a class discussion ensued pertaining to the field of biochemistry and the process of assimilation. Even though the majority of students had already taken chemistry, they seemed amazed by the simplistic concept of elements being recycled in such a natural, biological process. Jamal pointed out that a wastewater treatment plant is nothing more than nature "sped up." He said, "We use our technology to mimic what happens in nature. The difference is that we have concentrated the waste into one area and that is why we have to apply our knowledge of physics in order to increase the rate of these natural processes."

"Cool," said many of the students as Jamal displayed what looked like bright fluorescent lights shining through relatively clear water. Jamal said, "At this stage of wastewater treatment, the majority of the solid and organic material has been removed from the influent. During this process pathogens or disease-causing organisms are sterilized. The top three answers are on the board. Name a property or characteristic of this wavelength of light." The students really enjoyed this question as they had recently studied electromagnetic energy and its properties. "Exposure to these wavelengths can be harmful to living systems including humans," responded the student that provided the number one answer.

That was already a lot to cover in one class but Jamal wasn't done. There were ten minutes left and he was able to show the class a brief documentary that outlined the basics of wastewater treatment (Liu, S. X., 2014). Everything that was in Jamal's game was reviewed in the video. Jamal reminded the students about their homework and said that tomorrow would be a bit more traditional. They groaned. I randomly asked two of the students to remain after the bell. "How do you like physics?" I asked. "This is my favorite class," said one student. "My friends warned me not to take it because it was just another math course but they had a different teacher. Everything we do in here makes sense." "Why is that?" I asked. The second student replied, "Our teacher shows us why we are learning it. Today was a great example. I still remember the day he showed us how to estimate the height of a bridge using a stone and our phone's stopwatch. It's cool to know how to use what you learn in school." I thanked the students for their time and walked over to Jamal who was setting up for his next class. I told him, "The kids really love what you're doing." Jamal responded, "Not as much as I love what I'm doing." That was the number one answer!

Justin was very pleased with how his students had performed on their free body diagram assessment. They had proven that they had mastered the concepts and were able to identify forces acting on an object in two dimensions. Justin believes reviewing an exam with the students is crucial to establishing the importance of the assessment. While going over the test, a student asked, "Other than figuring out the force, what are some applications of determining tensile strength of a material?" That was a pretty easy question for Justin and he had no problem explaining that knowing the tensile strength allows engineers to determine the durability of a material and whether it will or will not perform adequately for its intended purpose. He offered several examples including materials strength in building construction, orthopedic implants and prosthetics in medicine, and energy storage and conversion devices in the field of technology. His answer to the student's question was certainly accurate and informative but Justin felt that something was missing. The students accepted the answer too readily and posed no more inquiries.

When he was finished Justin told the class, "That was the answer that I would have received from my physics teacher. I expect more from myself as your physics teacher." The class looked at Justin as if they had said something wrong. Realizing that his statement was not very clear, he said, "The Earth you are inheriting will have different problems than the planet my generation was given. Have your biology teachers ever discussed the field of biomimicry with you?" Many students either shook their heads or shrugged their shoulders. "Obviously not," said Justin. "I recently heard a presentation on biomimicry and thought of you guys working on tensile strength. Biomimicry is the science behind understanding how nature does things and then attempting to copy those processes as we design and produce materials." "Yes, I've heard of that," called out one student. "Is it true some spider webs are actually stronger than anything that human beings can make?" "I'm not exactly sure," replied Justin. "I'm not an expert on biomimicry or spider webs but that is what I was thinking about."

Justin spent a few minutes explaining that humans have certainly made remarkable achievements throughout history. "We consider ourselves the most intelligent form of life on the planet. Wouldn't you agree?" he asked the class. "These breakthroughs have provided the lifestyle that we enjoy today. In fact, the course that you are taking with me is a summary of the information that people have gathered in the field known as physics. I'd like to ask you a question. How many years of observing, hypothesizing, experimenting, and theorizing have human beings put into the combined sciences throughout history?" The students offered their answers with, "10,000 years" being the longest. "Okay," said Justin, "just to make a point, let's say that humans, or their ancestors, have been working on developing energy efficient processes for making stuff for 10,000 years. How long has nature, through the process of evolution been working on the same things?" "Whoa," said one student, "Billions!" "That's right," replied Justin. "Remember when you mentioned the strength of a spider's web. Nature has had millions of years to perfect that process. Don't you think we can learn a little bit about improving tensile strength by examining how spiders do it?" "That's so cool. I never thought of that," said one student. Justin responded, "Until recently, neither did many scientists. Let's try something fun. For homework, research an application of biomimicry that people are using to improve a process or substance. It doesn't have to pertain specifically to physics but would be great if it did. Please be prepared to share what you find with the class."

The next day Justin was thrilled to see the incredible level of enthusiasm being displayed by his class. The students were observed sharing and discussing their findings with each other before the bell even rang. "I can see that most of you enjoyed last night's assignment," said

Justin. "All you had to do was look it up on your phone," said one student. "There is tons of information on biomimicry. Why haven't any of our teachers ever told us about it?" "Actually" said Justin, "it's most likely because biomimicry is a new science. They had never learned about it when they were going to school." Justin then asked, "Would anyone like to go first?" Almost every hand went up.

The student presentations were outstanding. Topics included: competition swimsuits mimicking the effect of "dermal denticles" of a shark's skin; devices that help people climb by applying the manner in which geckos use tiny hairs on their feet to scale surfaces; wind turbines that are designed using the angle of attack similar to that of a humpback whale; extracting water from the air as does a species of beetle that lives in the African desert; applying the aerodynamics associated with the beak of a particular bird species to reduce the noise emitted by the world's fastest train; applying a woodpecker's method of shock absorbing techniques to improving safety during car collisions; a device capable of detecting its surroundings and changing color using a camouflage process similar to that of certain species of octopus; and the bending of light to create color in place of using potentially hazardous pigments, for this we can thank the peacock and its beautiful feathers (Hanks, T. W., & Swiegers, G. F., 2012).

There were many other interesting applications that were also presented and discussed. I certainly enjoyed learning of them and also observing the genuine appreciation that the students were showing for science. Many of the presenters made direct connections between their applications and what they had already learned in physics class. Justin obviously appreciated that. At the conclusion of the presentations Justin said, "You all did an incredible job. I hope that you are realizing that the concepts you learn about in physics may either be applied, or have something applied to them in order to make a positive difference." Justin explained that, he too, performed a bit of research. He investigated the spider's web and found that it has a tensile strength of 1.3 GPa while steel's is 1.65 GPa. This seemingly states that steel is stronger than a spider's web. However, a given weight of the spider's silk is five times as strong as the same weight of steel. Justin clarified, "This means that pound for pound, the actual silk of a spider's web is stronger than steel" (Sohn, E. 2014).

Some traditional physics teachers might argue that Justin lost a day of covering the curricular content by addressing biomimicry. However, had they witnessed the level of student engagement, the connections being made to physics, and the higher-order thinking that we observed during the class, I'm confident they would waste no time learning how to mimic Justin's lesson.

The curricular goal of Peggy's next unit was mastering the fundamentals of waves and sound. Fortunately, Peggy recently participated in our introductory seminar in which we expose teachers to the field of noise pollution and its control. She realized that noise would be the perfect, real world application through which she could teach nearly every aspect of her curricular content.

Donning earplugs and noise reducing headphones, Peggy appeared much better prepared for class than her students. They arrived to the sound of blaring music from her generation, and obviously, no student was wearing personal protection. "Dancing to music of the 80s today?" asked one of the students. "Oh good," yelled Peggy over the sound, "you consider this music. I consider what you listen to these days, noise." "Hey, I like our music," said one young man. Peggy reduced the volume and said softly, "That's why it is music to you and not noise. Noise is any unwanted sound," said Peggy. Unfortunately, she really set herself up as a "class comedian" exclaimed, "I get it. So, noise is what we hear when you talk about physics." Peggy shot him a "you got me" grin and said, "Literally, you may be correct but what I really mean is that noise is sound that can cause harm, either physically or psychologically to human beings."

Peggy turned the music off and showed the class a video of a tree falling down, however, she completely muted the sound. Peggy said, "Let's consider the age-old question. If a tree falls in the woods and nobody hears it, is there a sound? Before you answer, also consider a second question. If a tree falls in the woods and nobody hears it, is there a noise?" The students did not immediately offer an answer so Peggy repeated the questions and said, "There is a slight difference between a noise and a sound. Would anyone like to try to explain it?" One student offered, "I think that a sound is when molecules hit each other allowing energy to move in waves. However, in order for a sound to also be a noise, a person must hear it." "That's correct but can't a person also hear a sound?" asked Peggy.

"Yes, but if the person doesn't like the sound it's a noise," clarified the student. "Now you've got it," said Peggy, "In physics, we consider sound to be an objective quantity whereas noise is more subjective."

Peggy used an effective visual aide that modeled longitudinal sound waves emanating from a bell and eventually being received by a human ear. Peggy could see that the students were interested and said, "I will explain how we hear, but first, let's take a look at the basic principles of sound." Just as she would have typically done, Peggy introduced her students to the concepts of amplitude and frequency, commonly referred to as loudness and pitch. This time, however, Peggy wanted to connect these concepts to something that would relate directly to her students and their lives.

Peggy began by explaining how loudness or amplitude of sound waves is measured using a unit of pressure called the decibel (dB). She defined the scientific term for her students and then displayed a decibel or loudness scale on the touchscreen. The scale provided examples of common activities and the corresponding loudness expressed in decibels. She then held a device the size of a large smartphone near her mouth and said loudly, "Ahhhhhhh!" She looked at the device and said, "Good, about 80 decibels." "Whoa, that can tell you how loud you are?" enthusiastically asked a student. "Why don't you give it a try?" said Peggy.

Peggy briefly showed the student how to read the sound level meter and asked him to sing a note. Although it wasn't too pleasing to the ear, the student did his best "Ahhhhhhh" and said, "I beat you, 83 decibels." For several minutes, the students enjoyed measuring the loudness of different sounds. Eventually, Peggy explained that the sound level meter is only capable of measuring the rapid changes in air pressure or oscillations of molecules that we call sound. She went on to say that the device does not measure noise. Noise can only be qualitatively determined. Peggy tried to clarify by saying, "If someone yelled in your ear and you felt pain, the device may read 120 decibels of pressure but you might say that it hurt." The class engaged in a discussion involving the related experiences that students have had. The terms loudness, amplitude, pressure, decibels, sound, and noise were used often and appropriately (Lang, W.W., 1981). Peggy was more than satisfied with the dialogue.

"Let's move on to the next property of sound," Peggy said as she again displayed the visual of the ringing bell and ear. This time, the speed of the waves changed as did the frequency or pitch of the sound coming from the bell. "Do you hear how the pitch gets higher as the waves speed up?" asked Peggy. "That's why we refer to this property as frequency. The more often the waves pass per second, the higher the frequency or pitch of the sound." The application that Peggy was using allowed the students to alter the speed of the waves and observe the changes in frequency.

Peggy explained how frequency is measured in a unit called Hertz, abbreviated (Hz), which means waves per second. She told the students, "Humans with very good hearing can detect sounds between 20 to 20,000 Hz. Dogs can hear frequencies higher than 20,000 Hz and that is how a dog whistle works." I had to laugh when I heard a student say, "This is so much better than learning physics." Peggy also laughed as she proclaimed loudly, "This is physics!"

Peggy spent a few more minutes explaining that the properties of amplitude and frequency apply to all types of waves in varying mediums. She did say that electromagnetic waves, which will be covered later in the course, are a little different because they travel through a vacuum and do not depend on the movement of molecules. Peggy assigned some reading for homework and promised that the next day they would discuss how we hear, the problems that noise causes, and ways to protect ourselves from unwanted sound.

Peggy began the next period by displaying the original visual of the bell, sound waves, and human ear and said, "Yesterday, one of you stated that the topic we were discussing was so much better than learning physics." Peggy smiled at the girl who had made the comment and received a smile in return. She continued, "In order to reinforce the relevance of this topic to physics, I am asking you to say the word 'physics' whenever you feel a statement pertains to something you had learned, or think you will be learning in class. Okay, let's discuss how we hear."

Peggy started the animated model and pointed to the electrical cord leading to the bell. She began by saying, "Electrical energy is transformed into the mechanical energy of the hammer hitting the bell." "Physics," shouted the students. Peggy looked up at the class, smiled, and then said, "The mechanical energy is then transformed into acoustical energy as the molecules of air compress and refract, moving the energy forward through the medium." "Physics," again yelled the class. "Too loud, turn down the decibels," instructed Peggy. "Physics," whispered the class. Peggy paused and said, "The acoustical energy is then transformed back into mechanical energy as the eardrum moves back and forth. Before you say 'physics' again, can anyone tell me how fast the human eardrum can vibrate?" "20,000 times per second?" offered one student. "Wow, somebody is really paying attention. You're right because that is the highest frequency that humans can hear."

Before Peggy could continue, a young man raised his hand and politely said, "Physics!" Peggy agreed, but added, "Obviously, all of you now realize how important a working knowledge of physics is to understanding sound and noise. You no longer need to say physics, okay?" The students laughed as Peggy continued, "In the inner ear, the mechanical energy is transformed into electrochemical energy and signals are eventually sent to your brain via the auditory nerve. Your brain then interprets these signals as sound."

The class spent several minutes discussing the characteristics of sound propagation and the particulars involved in the process of hearing. Peggy then went on to explain the problems associated with loud sound (Kunicki, R. 1987). She introduced the concept of noise-induced hearing loss, explained how it happens, and why a hearing aid may not always help a person with this condition. She also covered other physical and psychological effects that noise can have on human health. She detailed the physics behind personal hearing protection and sound cancelling headphones.

The student inquiries poured in and they seemed riveted to Peggy's presentation. One student asked, "How do you know all of this?" Peggy turned to me and said, "I recently participated in a workshop that demonstrated the connections between physics and environmental science. I did a little research on the topic of noise to get myself up to speed." "Well, this was great, and I'm glad you did that," said the student that originally inquired about the relevance to physics. The bell was about to ring so Peggy handed out a worksheet for homework that required the students to summarize the physics concepts covered in class. The handout listed page numbers so that students could refer directly to them in their text.

After class, I told Peggy that I felt as if I was listening to an expert audiologist. She explained that since her mother suffers from sensori-neural hearing loss she had a vested interest in doing the research and extra incentive to plan the lesson. Peggy said, "I'm amazed by how simple it was to infuse this information into the curriculum. I feel like I was actually able to cover more material in less time. Maybe it's because the students were motivated. I didn't feel as if I needed to force them to learn, they simply wanted to." I said, "That's the message that we are trying to get out there. It's a win-win for everyone. Hopefully, more teachers will HEAR about what you're doing!" My associates and I left that session feeling quite optimistic about our mission.

At a recent seminar, Rita shared one of her success stories that demonstrated how she infuses environmental concepts into her instruction. She explained that her class was studying simple machines. The lab tables were covered with levers, pulley systems, and gear setups that allowed the students to conduct their experiments. The curricular goal was to determine work input, work output, and efficiency. Rita was facilitating a review discussion when one student said that although it's not exactly a simple machine, he had heard of something that does have to do with energy efficiency. He asked her if new buildings are capable of using the sun to generate heat. Rita told him that was a great question and yes, they are called green buildings and utilize passive and active solar energy to provide their own heating and cooling. She discussed the LEED (Leadership in Energy and Environmental Design) certification program and explained how the goal of that organization is to help people construct buildings that are environmentally responsible and use resources wisely (U.S. Green Building Council, LEED, 2019).

Rita said she loves it when her students become motivated, take the initiative, and drive the learning process. She could see that the opportunity existed for a successful student-driven activity focusing on green design, and since she was at a transition point in her curriculum, she decided to allow the students to investigate the topic further. She posted the assessment date for the upcoming exam on simple machines and explained that they would be working on another project for the next two class periods. She instructed the students to prepare any questions they might have pertaining to simple machines for homework and that she would make answering those questions a top priority.

Rita had the class conduct Internet research on green buildings. She suggested they start by looking up the U.S. Green Building Council or USGBC. She organized the class into teams and challenged them to design their own eco-friendly buildings. She encouraged them to use their imagination and creativity, however she required them to provide evidence supporting that any technology they utilize in their building is feasible and proven effective. Each group was provided a large poster and colored markers to assist in developing a visual aid for their presentations.

Considering that the students were allotted only one in-class session to develop their designs, Rita described the deliverables as quite impressive. As the students worked on their posters, Rita circulated throughout the room and provided guidance on the scientific principles involved in green technologies, however she was careful not to provide creative assistance.

Properly identified by all of her students was the first component of green buildings, the use of materials derived from natural, renewable sources. Rita added that these materials must be obtained in a sustainable manner and if possible, from a nearby site to reduce the energy costs associated with transportation. She was pleased that many of her students required that their buildings be made of the highest percentage possible of reclaimed or recycled materials. She said that some of the groups even included a requirement that their materials meet certain LEED standards for energy, durability, recycled content, and waste minimization.

Rita summarized the second requirement of green buildings as eco-efficient energy systems. All student teams included passive solar design systems in their buildings. She said she enjoyed hearing them discuss and debate the size of the windows, the direction that they must face, and the necessity of "thermal mass" to absorb, store, and distribute the heat. Rita said it was rewarding that the young man who had asked her about the use of solar energy to heat buildings was able to answer his own inquiry. Many of the groups included requirements for high levels of insulation and energy-efficient windows. The majority of teams specified that all lighting and appliances meet certain energy-efficiency ratings. All groups selected and described some form of renewable energy resource to power their buildings. The most common sources were wind and solar, however, one group decided to use geothermal energy and another specified tidal energy. They explained that their buildings were to be developed in areas capable of harnessing those resources.

Rita then described how her students incorporated water management programs into their facilities. Most teams provided schematics for rainfall collection strategies that would be used directly for "gray-water" operations such as toilets and lawn irrigation systems. Students included other water management features in their buildings such as low-flow showerheads, water efficient appliances, and on-demand water heating. One group went so far as installing waterless composting toilets but later decided to go with low flush toilets based on the expected use of their facility.

Rita told us that she had recently been to Rome and was amazed at how efficiently and effectively that ancient civilization had harvested water. She smiled and admitted that she was planning to spend a little time showing her students pictures from that trip and that she would use a presentation on how these people used cisterns and paved courtyards to capture rainwater and supply the city's aqueducts as her justification.

Another component that all of the students included in their presentations was the requirement that the building be healthy to live in. The students set standards for indoor air quality by requiring the use of non-toxic building materials that were moisture and mold resistant. They also included LEED approved ventilation systems that would draw in fresh outdoor air and be capable of controlling humidity.

Two of the groups added one more important feature. Rita explained these students realized that in order to be feasible, the building must also be cost-effective. Rita said she commended them for providing support for their statement such as the cost reduction due to energy savings, positive economic effect on the local workforce, and the ability of the building to meet local community needs.

When Rita was finished sharing her experience she added, "Although the class enjoyed investigating the topic, the project was really special for me because I knew it was initiated by the students themselves." She went on to tell us that the students performed very well on their simple machines assessment proving that this slight deviation from the set curriculum had no detrimental effect on student performance. In fact, she believes that it was a welcomed break that may have served to rejuvenate their interest. She mentioned that many students asked her why she did not include any questions about green buildings on the exam. Rita told them that there was no need to. She said, "The test on green design is one that your generation will need to take together in the very near future." She told them not to worry and that based on how well they were all doing in physics, she was sure they would ace it.

Nick admits that he has always had difficulty teaching the laws of thermodynamics. He claims that the majority of his students never showed much interest in the topic. For this reason, along with his newly found appreciation for environmental science, Nick thought he would try something a little different and infuse some sustainability education into his introductory lesson.

Nick began the class by providing his students with the classic definitions of the laws of thermodynamics. "Generally speaking," Nick said, "The first law of thermodynamics tells us energy cannot be created or destroyed, only transformed. The second law states that disorder or entropy always increases in a closed system. The third law maintains that as temperature nears absolute zero, entropy levels approach a constant value since there would be no molecular motion." Nick then described a group activity to his students that would require them to investigate the relevance of these laws to the overall health of our planet. "I'd like you to look at how we use energy as well as our ability to sustain our way of life and relate that to the first two laws of thermodynamics." On the surface, the assignment may seem a bit daunting, however, the students did not seem at all deterred. Instead, they immediately set to task and began their Internet searches.

As Nick circulated among the students, he observed several of the groups creating categories for "First Law" and "Second Law" examples. He was surprised at how quickly these lists began to grow. A few minutes into the activity a student asked, "How detailed do we have to be?" Nick replied, "That is up to you. Be as detailed as necessary in order to fully make and support your statement." After about twenty minutes Nick asked, "Does anyone need more time?" One student said, "Actually, I think we could spend a year working on this." Nick agreed with the student but explained that he was just trying to make a quick point today and introduce them to a very important topic in physics.

Nick then led what can best be described as an extremely high-order dialogue involving energy flow and sustainability. One group began the discussion by saying, "Sustainability basically means to have the capability of continuing. Our society cannot keep going the way that it is." Nick interjected, "What does this have to do with the laws of thermodynamics?" Without hesitation, a young man from the group said, "Everything. Our society needs high quality energy to sustain itself. We transform high quality energy into low quality energy so although energy is not created or destroyed, we are moving to a state of disorder." The group went on to describe how fossil fuels represent a very high-quality form of stored energy. They explained how burning these fuels releases the energy that we use to power our society's needs and eventually, these high-quality fuels will be depleted. In the process, we transform the energy into heat that is primarily lost to the universe. They explained that transitioning to renewable energy would be a way that we could prolong our society and become sustainable as long as the sun continues to shine. "That was very good," said Nick, "Who would like to go next?"

The second group agreed with the first but provided a different type of example. They discovered what Garrett Hardin termed, "The Tragedy of the Commons." The team described how energy must be put into a system to maintain order otherwise the second law of thermodynamics would apply. They demonstrated how the human species continues to transform the Earth to suit its own needs and fails to restore the planet back to its original form. They asked the class if they ever looked at the cafeteria tables as they were leaving the room. There were audible chuckles as the class agreed that the tables were usually a mess. "That is because no one takes responsibility for the disorder. That is an example of the tragedy of the commons," said the group. "This tragedy occurs on a global scale," they continued. "Humans are degrading the soil, air, and water and since these are shared resources, no one is taking responsibility for the disorder. We believe that this is a clear example of the second law of thermodynamics. When you consider that much of the terraforming, we do is powered by fossil fuels the first law applies as well." "Terrific," said Nick.

The third group said that they looked specifically into one particular characteristic of our society, transportation. They maintained that our current forms of transportation are not sustainable. They said that not only do the majority of our methods of travel rely on fossil fuels but they also create pollution and contribute to enormous amounts of solid waste, much of which is not recyclable. As a result, the amount of disorder or entropy on our planet increases. They offered strategies in green technology as possible solutions to slow down the effects of the second law of thermodynamics. One of the students from the team said, "Did you know that there are cars that can be powered by the sun, water, and compressed air?" "Compressed air?" another student asked. "Yes, look it up. They are called compressed air vehicles and they run by releasing pressurized atmospheric air in a pneumatic motor," replied the group. Nick was especially pleased to hear they discovered that one of the problems with these vehicles is that the energy transformation is not very efficient. In other words, the first law of thermodynamics is creating a problem that future scientists will have to solve if this technology will someday be able to replace our gas-reliant modes of transportation.

Group four focused on deforestation and resource depletion. "Take a look at this," said one student as he pointed to his laptop screen that showed an aerial photograph of two adjacent countries. A classmate said, "One side looks like a forest and the other looks like a desert." "No," said the group, "The country that looks like a forest has environmental laws that protect its natural resources. The other country decided to sell off its resources. Now they are struggling economically." The team went on to explain that the two countries serve as a reminder that we cannot escape the first two laws of thermodynamics. They said that if we take the easy way out and rapidly reduce our high-quality energy for immediate economic gain we will suffer in the end because we will be in a state of disorder. They maintained that it is better for us to sacrifice a little now so that we can continue to live sustainably. "You guys are really making me think," said Nick.

The fifth group provided the class with the example of a coral reef off the Florida Keys that had been studied for years. They asked the class to consider that everything on the planet is connected. The first law of thermodynamics states that energy cannot be created or destroyed but how the energy moves through the system is also important. The change in our planet's overall temperature is altering the energy flow through these systems. The biological coral respond to this by expelling algae and eventually die. The group showed two pictures of the same coral reef taken nearly three decades apart. "Look at what our transforming of energy has done to this ecological system in only 30 years. Coral reefs are very complicated and dynamic systems of species that are all interconnected and reliant on each other for survival. We think that this is an example of disorder caused by our interference with the laws of thermodynamics." Nick bowed his head and said, "Thank you, that was very well done."

The last group examined human population and maintained that we are trying to defy the second law of thermodynamics. "People are always finding new ways to feed the world's human population. We are well past our carrying capacity yet we continue to adjust the environment to suit our own needs," said the group. They explained that although it may seem we are creating more order and defying entropy, this goes against the laws of physics so they warned, "If we keep this up, eventually something will have to change, and that might mean some type of catastrophe for our species." "I wish I could say that you are wrong, but I can't. This shows great insight," said Nick.

I really enjoyed observing this class because it is clear that Nick's students were creatively engaged at a very high level. I asked Nick if he thought these students would ever forget their introduction to the laws of thermodynamics. Nick said, "I can't believe it took me so long to figure something like this out." He thanked me for introducing him to the concept of infusing environmental science into the instruction. I told him that he is the one who should be thanked. All we did was introduce him to the environmental concepts. He was the one that found a way to relate those fundamentals to his curriculum. As we were leaving Nick said, "I think that even I am seeing the laws of thermodynamics a little clearer. I'll never introduce these laws any other way."

Mace's students told us that they really enjoy his class. That is not surprising since he is known for his creative and interesting hands-on lab activities. Mace was wrapping up his unit on light and its properties. When the students arrived to class, they were happy to see their teacher had another exciting activity planned. Examining the materials on the front desk, one student asked sarcastically, "What are we doing today, building a greenhouse?" Mace laughed and said, "How did you know?" The student shot him a look of astonishment. "Yes," Mace said, "I think it's important that you understand how a greenhouse works. If we build one, you will have a better understanding of how electromagnetic energy transforms into heat. You will also appreciate why scientists are so concerned about greenhouse gases and the effect that they have on global warming and climate change."

Mace had obtained several "do-it-yourself" greenhouse kits that he distributed to his students. He directed them to work in groups and handed out the project instructions. The students had the mini greenhouses assembled quickly and Mace said, "We are now going to use these greenhouses to grow our own plants in class. However, what I really want you to understand is how physics and environmental science relate to this process."

He began the lesson by showing an animated model on his touchscreen. The application projected an image depicting electromagnetic waves originating at the sun, traveling through space, into the atmosphere, and eventually hitting the outer glass of a greenhouse. Inside the greenhouse, the image of the waves changed from a violet, transverse pattern to a reddish, cloudlike form. Mace pointed to the image of the reddish cloud and explained that it represented heat energy. He said that the energy transformation occurs when the plants absorb the electromagnetic waves. Mace asked, "What do you notice about the heat?" A student responded, "It looks like it can't go through the glass as easily as the light energy does." "Very good," said Mace. Mace described how the light energy passes straight through the windows but the heat gets "trapped" by the glass and that is the basic physics behind how a greenhouse works. "Even in cold weather, as long as there is sun, greenhouses are warm. It's a form of passive solar heating," said Mace.

Mace turned the students' attention to a second image that was similar to the first. In this picture, however, the planet Earth appeared in place of the greenhouse. "What do you see happening here," asked Mace. The class watched the animation for a moment before a student raised his hand and said, "The Earth's atmosphere is acting like a huge greenhouse. It looks like the electromagnetic rays go right through the atmosphere, transform into heat energy and then can't get back out into space." "But there's no glass, what is preventing the heat from escaping?" Mace asked. One student pointed to the pictures representing molecules of methane, carbon dioxide, and water vapor and said, "These molecules are absorbing the heat and act like the glass in a greenhouse."

Mace praised the class for their efforts and then asked, "So what is the big deal that scientists are making over greenhouse gases?" A young lady quickly responded, "We are burning fossil fuels and that creates greenhouse gases like carbon dioxide. The Earth is heating up and that is going to cause problems for our planet's ecosystems. If we don't start transitioning to renewable energy sources, we are going to suffer the consequences of climate change." Mace laughed and said, "That was so well said. You obviously understand the problem better than many adults. How do you know all of this?" The student explained that she has taken the Advanced Placement Environmental Science Course offered at her school. "How many of the rest of you have taken or plan to take that course?" Mace asked. Not many hands went up. Mace shook his head disappointedly and said that he wanted to share a quick success story with the class.

Mace described the atmospheric ozone layer and explained its importance to protecting life on Earth from the sun's harmful ultraviolet radiation. He showed a brief video clip that explained how life would never have developed on our planet without it. Mace told the class that in the 1970s, chemicals called chlorofluorocarbons or CFCs were widely used as refrigerants and in propellants. Mace recounted how scientists discovered that these chemicals were reacting with, and depleting the ozone in our atmosphere. He described how well countries throughout the world worked together to eliminate the use of CFCs. "Basically," Mace said, "the people of the world cooperated to avoid what could have been a catastrophe for the human species and perhaps, all life on Earth by simply replacing CFCs with other, less problematic substances" (Douglass, A., Newman, P. A., & Solomon, S., 2014).

Mace encouraged the students to do more research on how scientists were able to convince the world's leaders to make changes that would literally save our species. Mace did not have to wait long to hear the question that he hoped would be asked. A student said,

"Since all of the scientists agree that burning fossil fuels is causing climate change, why aren't all of the countries working to stop this? What's the difference between solving the ozone depletion problem and solving the climate change problem?" "Money," yelled another student. He added, "Substituting a different chemical for CFCs wasn't a huge economic sacrifice. It costs lots of money to transition to renewable or green energy sources and people do not want to make the sacrifice." Mace was able to determine that this student was also taking the AP environmental science class.

Mace was careful to keep politics out of the discussion. Instead, he facilitated a higher-order dialogue focusing on the sustainability of our way of life and the important role that science will hopefully play. One student appeared angry when she said, "The planet doesn't belong to old people, it belongs to us!" Mace seized the opportunity to point out why education is so important to the future of the planet and why it is imperative that his students learn that truth is only revealed through science. Mace pointed to the class and said, "One day, you will be making the decisions. For all of our sakes, please base those decisions on facts that are grounded in science."

Mace could see that class was about to end so he asked the students to check his website for the homework assignment that reinforced the day's activity. After the bell, the students were still discussing the concept of climate change and taking second looks at their greenhouses. One student was staring at his and asked Mace, "What good is a greenhouse if all the plants die?" Mace turned to me and said, "Only a student could put it so eloquently." I couldn't resist. I told him. "Of course, it's all simple physics."

Chapter 9 – Our Biological Clock

I love to tell a story about a special colleague who taught me a great lesson as to the importance of embracing science. During my first year as a high school teacher, I had the pleasure of working with Kate. She was a well-respected, veteran educator and an outstanding biology teacher. She proved to be an exceptional mentor and friend, however, she seemed to derive some twisted form of pleasure out of personally irritating me with ridiculous comments that were completely contrary to consensus science. I remember her telling me that the moon landing never occurred, the Earth was flat, global warming was a hoax, smoking doesn't cause cancer, and all kinds of other outlandish statements. However, not only did she refrain from sharing these ideas with her classes, her ability to effectively relate our world's real, environmental problems to the lives of her students was quite remarkable.

Being the "new guy" in the department and holding out hope that she was just trying to get under my skin, I never confronted Kate on these issues. Her taunting continued for most of my first year. One day Kate and I were both in the lab prep room. She smiled at me and said, "I can't believe you handle it so well. Don't my idiotic comments make you angry?" Surprised, I candidly responded, "Yes. I know you don't believe the things that you say, so why do you make those preposterous statements? I think that's irresponsible, especially for a biology teacher." She laughed and said, "I'm sorry Joe, but you seemed the perfect target." "Target for what?" I asked. She continued, "I wanted to start a debate." I smirked as I stated, "A debate that you couldn't win?" "Now that's where you are wrong. Somebody once said that it is hard to win a debate when your opponent is not handicapped by knowledge of the facts." Kate really piqued my curiosity. She then said, "You definitely know your stuff Joe, and nobody in this department understands environmental science as well as you, but don't think that you can always use science to win a debate. There are ways to discredit science, and some people have learned how to use this skill to their advantage. Let me show you how this is done."

For the next several minutes we debated the fact that people had landed on the moon. She created lies, refused to acknowledge accepted scientific fact, and manipulated the conversation with absolute precision. I was astonished at how convincing she was. By the end of that discussion, I started doubting that people had actually landed on the moon! Kate made me realize that teaching the scientific principles is important, however, it is equally important to instill in our students an appreciation for science and the moral and ethical responsibilities that we must have when applying it. I told Kate that I never really thought of that before.

Kate provided numerous examples of leaders who have distorted the truth and manipulated scientific facts to support their own agendas. She explained how unethical people often fabricate their own "facts" to use as alternatives to scientific data in order to support statements and conclusions that are self-serving. That was a great lesson for a first-year science teacher and one that I will never forget. Many years later, I assumed the role of science department supervisor. After welcoming me to my new position Kate asked me if I held any grudges for what she had put me through my first year. I asked her, "Does it even matter what I say since you already know the scientific truth?" We shared a laugh. We have been, and will always be close friends. She was truly a gifted teacher.

By trade, most biology teachers are already eco-literate so it is always a pleasure discussing sustainability issues with them. However, when asked about the infusion of environmental education into the instruction, I have found that many biology teachers are unaware that they are already addressing sustainability in their lessons. A great example was an activity that Rachel had been using for years during her unit on species interaction. However, after attending one of our seminars, she made a little adjustment.

"Yes!" exclaimed several students when they entered Rachel's class and saw the setups on the back tables. "I've played that game," said a student as she pointed to one of the piles of small wooden blocks, carefully stacked to form one large rectangular tower. Rachel began her lesson by spending a few minutes reviewing ecosystems and species interactions. However, she could tell by the constant "head turning" that the students were eager to begin their lab.

"I think that many of you are familiar with the game that I have set up for you in the back of the room. However, before we begin, you will need to understand and know the difference between natural capital and economic capital. Can anyone tell me what is meant by economic capital?" One student said, "Isn't it how much money you have?" "That's close," said Rachel, "can anyone add to that?" A second student said, "I think it also has something to do with being able to survive hard times like a market crash." Rachel thanked the students and explained that both were correct. She told them that the more economic capital a company or organization has, the more capable it is to sustain its operations during times when money is tight.

Rachel asked, "So what do you suppose natural capital means?" "Nature's ability to withstand hard times?" offered a student. "True, but how does nature get that ability?" asked Rachel. The class seemed to have a little more difficulty answering that question so Rachel said, "Think about what we have been discussing in class." A student said, "Oh, the different species are like money. The greater the number of different species an ecosystem has, the better will be its chances of surviving a catastrophe." "That's great," said Rachel. "Yes, the greater the species diversity or biodiversity, the more resilient the ecosystem will be" (Vellend, M. 2017).

Rachel defined biodiversity and made an analogy between species abundance and diversity in an ecosystem, and abundance and diversity of monetary assets in a company. She said, "People often say that biodiversity is like an insurance policy for an ecosystem." She then showed a detailed model of an ecosystem. Everything seemed to be interconnected with arrows. She added, "Remember, some species are more important to the sustainability of an ecosystem than others. Do you remember what they are called?" One student raised his hand and responded, "They're called keystone species. Without them, the whole system will fall apart." Rachel asked, "Why does this happen?" The student said, "There are no other species that are capable of filling their role or niche." "Good. I think you are ready," said Rachel.

Rachel led the class to the back tables and distributed the instructions for the game lab. Instead of simply taking blocks out from the bottom of the tower and placing them on the top, students were required to randomly pick a card from a deck and remove the corresponding color-coded blocks. Each block color represented a different species. Players were eliminated as they removed the blocks that caused the tower to fall. Students were provided specific guidelines for rebuilding the tower. They played until they determined a winner.

While the students were playing the game, some interesting discussions were heard. One dialogue focused on the reason that the blocks representing human beings were located at the top of the tower. Other students debated whether the game was one of skill, luck, or some combination of the two. Another discussion focused on the importance of species abundance verses niche as it pertains to natural capital. Obviously, the students were already making connections of relevance between what they were learning in class and the environmental consequences of irresponsible human activity.

After allowing the students to play several rounds of the game, Rachel instructed them to write down what they believed to be the goals of the activity. Rachel facilitated a discussion that formed the following conclusions: First, the game demonstrated that removal of one or more blocks will almost always affect others. This is similar to the removal of one or more species from an ecosystem; second, the tower eventually falls because players are constantly removing blocks. This is similar to the fact that human activity is causing the elimination of species from ecosystems; third, since one specific colored block represented an entire level, its removal caused an immediate collapse of the tower. This is similar to the removal of a keystone species; and finally, the students stated that when the tower falls, the blocks at the top are always affected. This is similar to the fact that humans will not be able to survive if ecosystems fail.

Rachel then showed a brief video clip that demonstrated the actual ecosystem changes of a rain forest area that was transformed into farmland. The video documented thousands of species that were affected by the project. One student said, "That's not right." Rachel responded by saying, "That is one way of seeing it, however, more people are now able to be fed. Could someone claim that this is simply progress?" "Think of the game," said another student, "If you keep taking blocks off the bottom of the tower eventually it will fall, especially if you add more to the top." The students had obviously gotten the point.

Rachel explained the concept of sustainability to the class and told them that human activity is certainly affecting the ecosystems around the world. She briefly described the different viewpoints that people have when it comes to the role that humans should play. Rachel explained that while some people view humans as the master species, having the right to transform the world without restriction, others believe that we are the world's "stewards" and are responsible for restoring the ecosystems that we disturb. In wrapping up the lesson, Rachael reminded the students of their homework assignment and asked them to complete and submit an exit ticket reflecting on the day's activity and the relationship between economic and natural capital.

Rachel was able to reinforce the curricular content goals while enhancing the learning environment by infusing concepts of sustainability. I asked Rachel if she had performed this lab activity prior to attending our training session. She said although she had been using this activity for years, she never before emphasized the relevance to sustainability and the ethical and moral responsibility that the human species needs to assume. She said, "Adding the sustainability component made the topic relevant to the students and their future. This seemed to motivate the students and raised the level of engagement." I mentioned earlier that I have found that most biology teachers are already infusing the concepts of environmental science. As Rachel demonstrated, a few small adjustments to include a component of sustainability education may go a long way. Give it a try!

◆◆◆

Sam's biology class was studying genetics. She felt that they had already mastered the fundamentals so she decided to examine a more advanced topic with them. Sam showed the class a video focusing on genetic engineering or genetic modification that demonstrated how scientists apply the field of biotechnology to directly manipulate an organism's genes. The video explained how genetic engineering is being put to use in industrial processes, energy production, medicine, and agriculture. The class discussion quickly turned to GMOs or genetically modified organisms. Her students were amazed to learn the extent to which people have manipulated natural processes to improve the quality and increase the abundance of food supplies (Biotechnology FAQs, 2019).

Sam could tell that the students were motivated to learn more about food production. Knowing that this was an opportunity to reinforce recently covered material, she decided to allow them to explore the topic further. She provided every student a laptop and asked each to spend a few minutes researching information pertaining to food and its production. The students were obviously engaged as they were heard discussing their findings prior to reconvening as a group.

In order to effectively facilitate the class discussion, Sam had one pupil list the topics that the students identified as interesting and worthy of further research on the touchscreen. Those issues included: advances in food production technology that have allowed humans to exceed their carrying capacity; food security's role in causing a disconnect between humans and nature;

the scientific consensus that food production strategies reliant on fossil fuels are not sustainable; high-input agriculture's contribution to degrading the planet and decreasing biodiversity; alternative food resources; and the debate over the use of GMOs. Sam then organized the class into six research teams and assigned each group one of the topics. She asked them to investigate their issue and prepare a brief presentation for the class.

The first group to present began by defining the term carrying capacity as the population of a species that can be supported by an environment. They explained that there are living and non-living factors that determine how many organisms of each species can survive and that food supply is one of the most important. They briefly described how human beings have used technology and scientific applications such as genetic engineering to increase their food security. The group said that although this sounds like a good thing, the truth is that humans have increased their population at the expense of other species. They also pointed out that the human population has been increasing at an exponential rate ever since we discovered how to increase our food production. They noted that in the last 100 years, the world's human population has increased from under 2 billion to over 7.5 billion. The team concluded that this exponential growth could not continue forever. They explained that, sooner or later, we must either curtail our food production efforts or find other ways to control population growth. After a brief dialogue as to the alternatives, the class agreed with the team's conclusion (Daily, G. C., & Ehrlich, P. R., 1994).

The second group described food security as the measure of a person's accessibility to food. They explained that our society has made such strides in food security that the majority of our nation's citizens do not even consider themselves to be part of nature. The team demonstrated that food security for a country results in a healthy population and corresponding strong economy. They described several political, technological, and scientific strategies that wealthy countries use to improve the food security for their people. They certainly convinced the class that food security is an issue that is taken very seriously on the global and national scale. They developed an interesting analogy between our use of natural resources to build an unnatural infrastructure and our use of those natural resources to develop unnatural food (Koning, N., 2017).

The third group described how the large-scale use of fossil fuels during the industrial revolution contributed to an increase in high-input agriculture. They described this method of food production as requiring large amounts of money, commercial fertilizers, and land to produce a few, or even one type of crop. They added that high-input agriculture relies on fossil fuels. They explained how the burning of fossil fuels releases greenhouse gases resulting in higher global temperatures and climate change. The team also mentioned that fossil fuels are non-renewable. For this reason, high-input agriculture cannot be considered a sustainable practice. The group identified several sustainable agricultural solutions that are less harmful to our environment but explained that they are much less profitable at this time (Short, R., 1999).

The fourth group picked up where the last one finished off. They focused on the environmental degradation being caused by high-input agriculture. The team elaborated on the potential hazards associated with chemical fertilizer manufacturing and pesticide use. They provided examples and showed powerful photographs of air, water, and soil pollution caused by modern agricultural practices. After briefly describing the importance of biodiversity, the team provided evidence that human beings are terraforming the planet to support only one species. They explained, although productive and efficient in the short term, continuing this selfish practice will result in the elimination of species, the destruction of ecosystems, and eventually, the end of the human life support systems on our planet.

Group five identified several alternatives to high-input agriculture. They described two methods of food production that rely on renewable energy from the sun and animal labor. They explained that although not as economically profitable, these strategies are less harmful to the environment and are also sustainable practices. The team described the practice of aquaculture or fish farming that may someday have a very positive impact on transitioning away from high-input agriculture. The group discussed the practice of hydroponics that involves the use of a nutrient-rich solution instead of soil to grow plants. They then added that if perfected, genetic engineering might hold the key to sustainable food resources (Alternative Farming Systems Information Center, 2019).

The last group tackled the issue of genetically modified organisms. They began by defining a GMO as a food made from soy, corn, or other crops grown from seeds that were genetically engineered to have a predetermined DNA and explained that there are pros and cons to their use. They listed the pros as giving the plants greater resistance to insects as well as a high tolerance to herbicides, heat, cold and drought. They explained that GMOs are capable of being modified to have better shelf life, more vibrant color, and higher levels of nutrients. The students then listed the cons as the possibility of triggering allergies, the potential link between GMOs and antibiotic-resistant bacteria, and controversies surrounding studies connecting cancer to the ingestion of herbicide resistant GMOs (Goyal, P., & Gurtoo, S., 2011).

Sam discussed the relevance of this activity to her students' studies in genetics and then to the overall field of biology. She told the class that sometimes it is better to examine the world as a whole and then work your way down to the smaller details. She told her students she was pleased they were able to demonstrate that they could connect what they were learning about in class to the larger issues that will need to be addressed in order to provide their generation with a sustainable world.

Sam should be commended for her classroom management and organizational skills. I told her that she did an exceptional job facilitating the learning and seemed to get the most out of her students' efforts in such a short amount of time. She told me that through the years she has learned to allow the students to do the "heavy lifting." "They would rather listen to each other than listen to me anyway," Sam said with a smile. Observing the quality of information that the groups provided and realizing how well they related what they were learning to the real-world issues, it was clear that she was making a good point. Perhaps Sam was spot on about allowing the students to do the heavy lifting. After all, when it comes to sustainability education, we are talking about an entire planet and we may need them to do most of the work!

Emily teaches high school biology. At one of our sustainability workshops, she was her team's science representative for an activity in which participants brainstormed infusion possibilities. Her group came up with an outstanding idea and collaborated to develop a workable implementation strategy. Emily took this theoretical activity to the next level by seeing her group's vision all the way through to fruition in her classroom.

For years, Emily has excelled at teaching the fundamentals of asexual cellular reproduction and mitosis. She will tell you the scientific intricacies involved in cell division and the problems that can occur with these processes are relatively straightforward concepts. However, understanding the manner in which these biological concepts, environmental conditions, and our society are all interconnected is something else and much more difficult for students to comprehend. When Emily's curricular goals progressed to the topic of cancer, or unchecked cell growth caused by mutations in genes, she decided to demonstrate the part that our physical and social environment plays in determining the risk of these mutations and the potential development of these afflictions.

As students entered class, they observed a statement on the touchscreen that read, "As a society, we often choose the level of cancer risk and potential death that is acceptable. Do you agree or disagree? Be ready to support your answer." Emily gave the class five minutes to write down their individual thoughts. She then asked the students to join with three other people to discuss their ideas. Emily soon initiated a class discussion on the topic. Immediately, one student offered, "I definitely agree with that statement because we are free to choose whatever we want to do. For example, I choose not to smoke so I lower my risk of getting lung cancer." In response to that statement, another student said, "Maybe, as an individual, you can choose to not smoke but what about a person who has no choice but to live or work near someone else who does smoke and is polluting the air? They do not get a choice."

Emily gained everyone's attention and said, "Those are both great points. However, did you ever think of this? People do have a choice during elections and they can vote for politicians promising to set limits on air pollutants such as carcinogens that constituents determine to be acceptable." Emily went on to explain that "acceptable risk" is a complicated societal topic. The students then became engaged in a higher-order discussion focusing on acceptable risk. Emily anticipated the high level of engagement that this dialogue would create and developed an activity for her students that would reinforce the complexities of the issue.

Emily kept the students in their groups. She told the class, "I am now going to hand out a set of cards to each group. There are six different categories so you will be getting a total of six cards." Emily circulated through the room, and to ensure that the distribution was random, allowed the teams to pick a card out of her hand for each category. The categories included: biology; toxins/hazards; route of entry/distribution; social; economics; and legal. Each card contained specific information pertaining to its corresponding category topic. Emily designed the activity so that regardless of the distribution sequence, a reasonable scenario could be created based on the connection of information contained on all six cards. After providing some basic guidelines, the student teams were challenged to develop a brief story that connected all of the topics specified on the cards that they had been dealt.

Students began by attempting to make sense of the information that they were provided. Groups were observed forming cause and effect relationships among the categories. Many team members were given research tasks while others discussed potential relationship scenarios. The short stories that the class delivered were the result of student knowledge, understanding, application, analysis, evaluation, and creativity; an excellent example of higher-order thinking.

The first group to present provided a representative sample of the class deliverables. Their scenario went something like this:

Nearly ten years ago, in a small town known as Tufluk, a group of citizens had lost a long and hard-fought battle with the local government over the zoning of a manufacturing facility in their town. The citizens were split over the issue as many had been promised jobs with the international company while others were concerned that the manufacturing process would contaminate the town's water, air, and soil. During the debate over zoning of the facility, lawyers for the company used predictive mathematical modeling to demonstrate that the unavoidable discharge of the chemical known as vinyl chloride presented what they termed an "insignificant risk" to the community. Eventually, the company received its permit and the facility became operational.

Several years later, a young boy was diagnosed with a rare form of liver cancer. Less than a year later, another child was diagnosed with brain cancer, a factory worker with lung cancer, and two cases of leukemia emerged. A group of concerned citizens began to investigate the unnaturally high incidence of these illnesses and the potential link that they believed to exist between those diseases and the factory operations. They discovered that vinyl chloride is considered a Group 1 Carcinogen according to the IARC (International Agency for Research on Cancer) and has been linked to all of the types of cancer they were seeing in their community. They found that the most common route of entry into the body for vinyl chloride is inhalation or by breathing the substance into the lungs. However, if the substance contaminates the water supply it can also get into the homes when people shower, cook, or do laundry.

The people of Tufluk were now in a panic. They filed a civil lawsuit against the company. They assumed that since the link between the recent cases of cancer and the facility was so obvious, operations would be shut down immediately. Unfortunately for the townsfolk, the legal issues were not as simple as they expected. Proving that the specific pollutant being discharged by the factory was the direct and sole cause of the problems of mitosis and cellular division occurring in a victim's body was nearly impossible. It was more a matter of percent possibility or probability.

Those filing the lawsuit had another problem to deal with. Many of their friends and neighbors were now employees of the company and relied on that factory as their primary source of income. The town of Tufluk was torn apart as the civil suit dragged on for several years. Eventually, the families of the cancer victims were awarded damages for their losses but the factory continued to operate. To this day, nobody knows if the high incidence of cancer was truly caused by the factory. Some people believe that the company had somehow illegally disposed of the vinyl chloride to save money in waste management costs but that was never proven.

The other groups developed stories that involved different chemicals, political and economic scenarios, and legal and social aspects yet they were all very similar when it came to the application of pure science in situations that involve probability and statistics. When all of the presentations were finished, Emily asked, "Not so easy when science meets the real world, is it?" One student said, "This was good though. It made us see how everything fits together. Sometimes that is hard to see when you are studying one small aspect of life like we sometimes do in science." "Are you saying that what we are learning in biology class is small and insignificant?" Emily said with a smile. "No," said the student, "I'm really saying the opposite. Studying something like mitosis and how cancer forms is very important but that gets lost sometimes in the real world." "That was very insightful," said Emily.

A young man raised his hand and said, "I saw a movie about something like this." He went on to describe the basic storyline but couldn't remember the name of the movie. Emily recognized the details and told the class that the movie was called *A Civil Action,* and was based on a true story (Zaillian, S., et. al. Buena Vista Home Entertainment, 1999). She augmented the student's account of the story and explained that she had always appreciated how the movie recounted the actual events from a scientific viewpoint while many of her friends enjoyed it for its legal and social components. She asked the students to raise a hand if they had seen the movie. Only a few hands went up. "Okay, it looks like I have to find some time for a movie, or better yet, I can see if your social studies teachers can show it and provide you with insight beyond my expertise," said Emily.

Emily discussed what she had done in class with the social studies supervisor. She was confident that she had met her goals for her curriculum but perhaps, teachers from his department might be able to further those efforts to explore this interdisciplinary topic in more depth and from a different viewpoint. He thanked Emily for her enthusiasm and promised to bring it up at their next department meeting. Emily shared that in the future, the biology and social studies teachers will be developing an interdisciplinary activity that will incorporate many of the strategies that she had used. For now, she decided to show

A Civil Action, and analyze the movie with her students to the best of her ability.

As I mentioned previously, Emily's lesson had all of the components necessary for developing higher-order thinking skills. Her enthusiasm carried over to the students and provided the motivation for them to drive the learning process. The fact that her students were able to relate and apply the curricular content to real world scenarios was outstanding. However, taking the initiative to share her students' success with her learning community was exceptional. Emily's students wrestled with the spread of cancer in a community. That is a terrible and scary thing. Emily is spreading the idea of infusing environmental education into the learning environment. I guess things that spread can also be wonderful.

Ben was introducing the process of photosynthesis to his students. They had recently learned that plants assimilate carbon dioxide and water, and in the presence of sunlight, convert these substances into sugar and oxygen. He posted the general chemical equation on his touchscreen and detailed the seven steps of photosynthesis that occur as carbon dioxide and water enter the leaf of the plant. He demonstrated how light energy is used to liberate oxygen and convert the carbon into carbohydrates.

One student asked, "Don't we have too much carbon dioxide in the air or something like that? Why don't the plants just remove it using photosynthesis?" Ben did his best to explain that although photosynthesis does work to reduce carbon dioxide emissions, the natural processes are unable to keep up with the magnitude of human disruption to environmental systems. Realizing that his students did not have a full grasp of the concepts, Ben recognized this as a good opportunity to expose the students to factual climate science and amplifying climate feedback loops.

Ben explained that atmospheric carbon dioxide levels are continuing to increase primarily due to the expanding use of fossil fuels. He used some visual aids to demonstrate how carbon dioxide and other greenhouse gases serve to warm the atmosphere. He explained that the increased temperature causes the ocean and soil to release more carbon dioxide and thus, we create an amplifying feedback loop. Ben briefly described the impacts of climate change, citing the frequency and intensity of drought, storms, and heat waves. He explained the cause and significance of rising sea level and ecosystem failure. Ben said, "For many years scientists have been warning us about climate change and the need for our society to transition to renewable energy that does not rely on the burning of fossil fuels. However, there are many reasons, mostly economic, that have prevented us from taking significant action" (Rapp, D. 2014).

Ben then described a hypothetical scenario in which our society, for whatever reason, fails to reduce its use of fossil fuels. He challenged his students to identify realistic ideas and strategies, aimed at reducing carbon dioxide levels in our atmosphere; ones that could break the current amplifying feedback loop and provide hope for a sustainable future. Ben provided some basic ground rules for the activity. One of those rules was that as soon as feasible emission reduction strategies were identified, the students were to list them on the board so that there would not be duplication.

The students took out their laptop computers and started investigating possible carbon dioxide reduction strategies. One by one ideas began to show up on the board (Overview of Greenhouse Gases, 2018). Solar and Wind Energy were the first strategies to be posted. Eventually, the list grew to read: "Solar Energy, Wind Energy, Carbon Capture / Storage / Sequestration, Nuclear Power, Biomass, Natural Sinks, Energy Efficiency, Green Transportation, Food Selection and Type, Water Management, Recycling, Photochemical Removal, Carbon Dioxide Capturing For Fertilizer, Recycling Carbon Dioxide Back into Fuels, Wetlands Reestablishment, Silvopasture, Regenerative Agriculture, Population Control. The students were still busy researching and posting when Ben said, "Wow, this is great. I wasn't even aware of some of these myself. Obviously, we can keep going but this should be enough to make our point."

Ben started the discussion by asking the students that listed alternative energy sources such as Wind, Solar, Nuclear, and Biomass, "How do these practices reduce carbon emissions if the burning of fossil fuels is not reduced?" They discussed the question briefly among themselves and then responded, "They will be able to keep the levels of carbon dioxide from increasing. Also, new technology should improve the efficiency of these sources. When that happens, people will transition over to renewable resources simply because doing so will be economically beneficial." "I can't argue with that," said Ben.

"So, what is Photochemical Removal?" asked Ben. A student explained that it is called photochemical carbon dioxide reduction and it is similar to photosynthesis. In the process, solar energy is used to convert carbon dioxide into other substances. He said the process uses a solar cell that mimics photosynthesis to convert carbon dioxide into a fuel (Magill, B., 2016a). "Interesting," said Ben, "and what about Carbon Dioxide Capturing For Fertilizer?" A student responded, "I read about a commercial carbon dioxide capture plant that converts the greenhouse gas into substances that can be used as fertilizer. They say that they plan to reduce one percent of global emissions by 2025" (Magill, B., 2017). Another student described Carbon Sequestration as a process by which carbon dioxide is captured then injected and stored into lava that solidifies (Magill, B., 2016b).

Ben was visibly pleased with the efforts of the students. "You are all doing a great job. What did you mean by Food Selection and Type?" asked Ben. The student responsible for posting that said, "Certain food sources such as meat and dairy require much more energy to produce than agriculture. Less energy use means less carbon dioxide in the atmosphere." Ben pointed to Energy Efficiency and the student who listed it said, "This is just common sense. The more efficient we are with our energy, the less fossil fuels will be burned, and the less carbon dioxide will be released." Another student interjected, "The same idea applies to mine which was Water Management." "My strategy is like that too," said the student who listed Recycling, "The more we recycle, the less energy we need to use and the less carbon dioxide we produce."

"What is Silvopasture?" Ben asked. "Instead of having open grazing lands you also have trees. This way there is more biomass able to absorb the carbon," responded the student. "A Natural Carbon Sink is anywhere carbon is stored. For example, there is trapped carbon at the bottom of the ocean and in our wetlands. People are working on ways to capture carbon dioxide and store more in these places," added another student.

"Am I safe in assuming that by Green Transportation you mean take the bike or walk?" asked Ben. "Yes," said a student as he added, "Transportation is one of the largest contributors to our global carbon dioxide levels. If you really think about it, we waste a lot of energy using cars. Had cars never been invented, and people relied on mass transit or human power for individual transport, this world would be in much better shape." "We can't forget about Regenerative Agriculture. That has to do with leaving biomass in the ground. Why release any more nutrients than we have to anyway?" interjected a student from the back of the room. A student then explained the last item on the board by saying, "As our population exponentially increases so does the amount of carbon dioxide that we pump into the air. Maybe if we can control our population, we will be able to stabilize our carbon dioxide emissions."

"You all did an incredible job. These are all excellent alternatives to our society's best option for reducing carbon dioxide levels, namely, eliminating our reliance on fossil fuels. In this class, we have certainly deviated a long way from photosynthesis, or have we?" asked Ben. He added, "Why do you think I asked you to perform today's activity?" One student said, "I think you wanted us to relate what we were learning in biology class to the real world." "That's true," said Ben, "but are all of the issues we discussed today related to biology?" The student said, "If there is one thing that I learned in biology this year, it's that everything is related in our environment." "Great point," said Ben.

Ben posted the homework and reminded the students to begin their studies for an upcoming assessment. I asked him if any of the concepts from today's lesson would be appearing on the exam. He told me that the students would be required to imagine and describe an atmosphere capable of supporting the human species in a world without plants. He laughed as he admitted he had not yet developed a rubric for that open-ended question. I asked him to let me know of the best responses. I told him that he might just hear the next great concept in the field of sustainability.

Brian wanted to motivate his students for their next major unit. They were going to study the biological systems (circulatory, digestive, endocrine, etc.) of the human body. To do this, Brian developed an activity that required his students to analyze a theoretical patient's symptoms and determine the toxin to which he or she was exposed, the route of entry into the body, and how the exposure may have occurred.

When the bell rang Brian said, "Welcome Doctors. Today will be the greatest challenge of your young careers." The students laughed. He arranged the class into six teams and distributed the activity handouts. Each group received medical reports for eleven hypothetical patients, Material Safety Data Sheets (MSDSs) and Hazardous Substance Fact Sheets (HSFSs) for eleven substances, and the details of eleven possible exposure scenarios. Brian said, "Your job is to match these eleven patients with the substance and exposure scenario that most likely caused their illness".

Brian circulated throughout the room as the students began to evaluate the information that they were given. They organized the materials into categories as they discussed possible correlations and potential scenarios that would account for the patient conditions. "Not so easy, is it?" asked Brian. "No, there is so much information," responded one student. "Well, just imagine how tough it is for the real physicians. At least I started you off with the materials you will need. Most of the time, doctors have to do all of the research on their own."

As the class progressed, students connected the three categories of information and began to construct plausible scenarios. One student said, "This is so interesting. It's like a game, but in a way, it's for real." "That's right," said Brian, "Exposures like this happen every day. The branch of science we are dealing with today is known as environmental toxicology. If we can trace illnesses back to the source, oftentimes we can prevent future exposures."

When it appeared that the students were ready, Brian asked, "Would anyone like to share a scenario that they feel confident about?" One group offered, "We think Patient #5 has mesothelioma and that he developed this illness from inhaling asbestos fibers at his workplace." "Correct," said Brian. A second group said, "Patient #9 has dermatitis brought on by direct skin exposure. We think he was exposed because he was not wearing the proper gloves at his job." Another group said that they were fairly sure that Patient #3 swallowed arsenic. They said, "The child has all of the symptoms of arsenic poisoning and most likely ingested this substance while playing in the kitchen of the family's home." Brian said, "You guys really do sound like doctors! Who thinks they figured out Patient #4? "We think that patient #4 was bitten by a snake while he was hiking," said a student. "We believe the venom contained a neurotoxin that affected several of his body systems and resulted in paralysis." "So far, it looks like you have been able to piece together the clues," said Brian as he handed out the answer key. He then allowed the groups time to compare and discuss their findings.

Brian said, "You all did a great job today. I'm hoping you gained an appreciation for the field of environmental toxicology. Does anyone have any questions before we tackle the major body systems?" "It was exciting to make these connections. It was like solving mysteries. Can we do this again?" a student asked. Brian said, "I'm glad you enjoyed it. I will try."

Brian had just enough time to display eleven body systems on the board. He briefly defined each and asked, "Did you notice that in our activity there were several possible scenarios for some of the patients?" "Yes, that's why doctors can never be completely certain of their diagnosis," said one student. Brian agreed and instructed the students to read the next section in their texts and told them that they would be starting with the circulatory system.

Brian wanted an effective strategy for motivating his students in learning the body systems. He accomplished much more than that with his activity. In addition to meeting his goal, his students analyzed environmental information, examined and compared systems of the body, and applied this knowledge to create real world cause and effect scenarios. This was an outstanding example of students practicing their problem-solving skills and the seamless infusion of environmental education into the instruction.

At one of our workshops, Krista shared that she was very pleased with her students' performance on their recent assessment on evolution. That is why she felt a pit in her stomach when a student asked, "Since the ice caps are melting, why don't polar bears just evolve to have gills and live in the water?" After addressing the answer to that question with her class, Krista was surprised to find out how many of her students were under the impression that species are capable of evolving in order to adapt to, and keep pace with changing environmental conditions. That day, in the faculty lunchroom, she shared what had happened in class with her colleagues and was equally amazed to observe that many of them were also unaware of the actual process by which species are naturally selected.

Krista demonstrated for us a card game that she had developed. She used it to aid her students in understanding the topics of adaptation and natural selection. The game consisted of a deck of cards with 80 different numbers on each card. Those numbers were random and ranged from 1 to 100. In other words, 20 numbers were missing between 1 and 100 on each card. These cards contained slightly different sets of numbers, and were called EC (Environmental Conditions) cards. Each player was also given one card called an S (Species) card that contained only one number between 1 and 100 representing a species and were referred to as Species Numbers. The original numbers on the S cards also appeared on every one of the EC cards in the deck. Every time an EC card was flipped over, a player was able to stay in the game if their Species Number on their S card also appeared on the EC card. Before each round in which a new EC card would be flipped, every player must roll a die and either add or subtract that value from the original number on their S card. This number (still between 1 and 100) becomes their new Species Number.

Those directions may seem a bit confusing but playing the game was quite simple. Basically, both the EC cards and the Species Numbers were changing. If a player's Species Number just happened to change so that it matched a number on the new EC card, the player continued. Krista explained that in a similar fashion, if a species gets lucky with an adaptive trait that is necessary or advantageous in their new environment, they "evolve."

If not, they become extinct. One member of the workshop group said, "What is the point of the game? It is very apparent that winning the game is purely a matter of luck." "That is exactly the point!" said Krista emphatically.

Krista explained that she was so engrossed in teaching to meet her curricular goals that her students failed to grasp the meaning and relevance of what they were learning. After revisiting the principles of evolution and demonstrating their relevance to changing environmental conditions, she found that the students were then able to make the connections to the real world. She made certain that her students understood that without human interference, species over very long periods of time would adapt to the ever-changing environmental conditions around them. In other words, there would be enough time for advantageous genetic mutations to occur that would allow species to "get lucky" and adapt to their surroundings.

Krista told us that after approaching the topic from the environmental viewpoint, she could see the students were able to realize that human induced climate change is creating environmental conditions for which life is not suited and natural evolution cannot keep pace. She said she was thrilled when the student who asked about the polar bears told her, "I get it now. Climate change is flipping the cards too fast and species aren't getting enough chances to roll the dice." The workshop attendees applauded Krista for her ingenuity. One participant said it best, "The world is changing and so is the way that we will have to teach. Thank you for proving that teachers are able to adapt."

◆◆◆

One of the slides that we use in our introductory presentation really struck a chord with Colin. As soon as he saw it, he knew that he was going to use it in his teachings. The slide displays two images, side by side. On the left appears the naked back of a man who is obviously suffering from some form of skin disease. On the right is a nighttime image of the Earth taken from the top of the atmosphere. It clearly displays our cities, urban sprawl, and other brightly lit signs of development.

Colin's biology class was studying disease-causing entities. They were learning about pathogens such as bacteria, fungi, protozoa, worms, and viruses. In recent weeks, the students had been assigned individual research projects and shared their findings in class discussions on the topics. Colin invited me to join his class on the day he planned to incorporate the slide we use at our workshop. It turned out to be well worth the trip.

To begin class, Colin displayed the images of the man and Earth on the touchscreen. He asked the students to simply study the images for a few minutes and jot down any thoughts they might have. He then organized the class into six teams and asked them to discuss their thoughts as a group and come up with a statement about the images that they could support. When it appeared that all of the groups had finished, Colin said, "Okay, what do you think about these two images?"

Three of the six groups focused completely on the diseased aspect of the man's skin. They attempted to identify the type of pathogen causing the illness by linking the man's symptoms with what they had already learned about disease-causing agents. They also described what they believed the skin ailment to be and proposed possible treatment options. Two of the three groups felt that the image of the Earth was placed side by side with that of the diseased man to symbolize the dominance that human beings have over the planet and to demonstrate that we have the technology and power to handle almost anything. In this case, the problem is one diseased person. The third group simply disregarded the image of the Earth. When asked directly about it they said, "We didn't think that the images had anything to do with each other. We just thought it was a beautiful picture of the Earth at night."

The remaining three groups all focused on the similarities between the two pictures. One group said, "We think the pictures are side by side to show that just like the man's skin, the Earth's surface is diseased." They went on to explain that based on what they had just learned in class, the human species is much like a virus. They described how a virus lives off a host in a manner similar to the way we live off the Earth. A virus takes what it needs at the expense of its host. They attempted to show that we do the same thing with the Earth's resources.

The next team added to the first group's analogy by saying, "When you look at the Earth's surface you can see the lights from space. Those lights aren't supposed to be there just as blisters are not supposed to be on the surface of a person's skin. The pustules indicate that something is wrong with the system. They are a result of something that needs to be corrected otherwise the person may eventually die. The artificial light that we see is a sign that something is wrong with our planet. It must be corrected or the planet may eventually die." The third group added that like a disease, the lights are spreading at an exponential rate and so are we. They also pointed out that electricity comes from using substances (fuels) that are found inside the Earth and that the pus forming on the man's skin originated from substances within his body. The looks on some of the students' faces and the sounds of disgust that they made in response to that comment were priceless!

Once order was restored, Colin explained that there were no right or wrong answers to what the class had been discussing and commented that all groups made valid statements and supported them well. Pointing to the slide Colin said, "I remember seeing those pictures for the first time and thinking that a dermatologist would definitely see a problem with the man's skin. However, I wondered if the doctor would view the Earth's picture as beautiful, as some of you did today. I guess it all depends on a person's point of view. I wondered what a planet doctor, if there was such a thing, would say."

The class became silent as everyone was observed staring at the images. "It does make you think, doesn't it?" asked Colin. He then directed the students to reflect on what they had been learning about in class saying, "In biology, we often study science on a very small, and sometimes microscopic scale. We should never forget that what we learn has relevance to the world and our universe."

Observing this lesson, I found it interesting how Colin's class was able to appreciate the analogy between human population growth and the spread of a simple virus.

It was refreshing to see that the viewpoints of all students were given equal merit and that discussions remained grounded in scientific fact. After class, I thanked Colin for inviting me to the lesson. I asked him how often he infuses environmental education into his instruction. He told me that he was about to say, "Ten times a year," but then he paused. "You know," he said, "I probably say or do something that promotes sustainability at least every few days. I just don't bring attention to it." I told him, "Most teachers do as well and don't give themselves credit. However, it is important that we take the time to demonstrate the relevance to our students." Colin looked at me, smiled and said, "I know because . . ." He paused. I asked, "Because why?" He looked at his watch and said, "Because our biological clock is ticking." That was so corny but how could you not love it? I had to ask him if it was okay for me to use that as a name of a chapter in my next book.

Chapter 10 – The Sustainable Arts

The arts are often the most unappreciated disciplines when it comes to providing opportunities to infuse environmental education into the instruction. However, nowhere is it more important to promote sustainability in the educational environment than in classrooms of the arts. These settings are havens for self-expression, and more importantly, promoting effective altruism. Effective altruism refers to finding ways of improving lives on a global scale. Never before in our history have young people been so passionate about saving their planet. It has been my pleasure working with teachers of the arts in allowing these future leaders the opportunities to display that passion and appreciate how others have done so before them.

There is another, more pragmatic reason for instructors of the arts to find ways to make environmental education an integral component of their lessons. By doing so, they demonstrate to their school leadership that the arts are also utilitarian in nature and necessary complements to the science, technology, engineering, and mathematics (STEM) programs. Unfortunately, many school leaders still view the different disciplines as separate and distinct. I must admit that my blood boils every time I hear an administrator say in regard to sustainability education, "Oh yes, they cover that in our environmental science course." In those instances, I try to remember that many of us think and act in accordance with those principles and values that have been ingrained in us through our own education. That is why today's educators must strive to break this destructive feedback loop that strangles interdisciplinary cooperation. This is certainly an issue that the arts are well prepared to address.

At one point in my administrative career, I was serving as supervisor for both the science and art departments for my district. It was district policy that faculty of similar instructional responsibility discuss important issues at least once per month in what were termed, "department meetings." Members of both departments were surprised when I combined the two faculty groups at the first meeting under my direction. It was not long before my colleagues realized the advantages of these meetings. Teachers recognized that we all shared common goals and by working together complemented each other's curricular objectives. Although that was many years ago, and at the time, none of us realized how progressive our actions were, our efforts had resulted in producing extremely well-rounded graduates. We can do the same in regard to creating truly eco-literate graduates.

◆◆◆

I first met Gabby at one of our introductory presentations. I distinctly remember her telling me, very respectfully mind you, that she had no idea why she was even signed up for the training since it had nothing to do with what she teaches. I enjoy reminding her of that and we always share a laugh about it. If you ever visited her art room, you would immediately understand why. Something inside Gabby came alive at that initial presentation. She claimed she found what she called a "dormant passion" that she never realized was hidden within her. She was moved by the mission of sustainability professionals and captivated by the field of environmental science. She referred to that science as "the art of sustaining beauty." Being a scientist all of my life, I never quite saw it that way. However, she had a good point. If one views our way of life as beautiful and applies science to keep it that way, I can certainly see why a person might consider that an art. I know that I often refer to teaching as more of an art than a science.

Gabby invited me to observe her students and see "environmental art" being created. As soon as we entered her classroom, we could feel the energy of expression beaming from the projects that filled the room. Not being an artist myself, I am having difficulty describing these projects. It might be more appropriate for me to say that they seemed to be shouting, "Our world is beautiful, we must take care of it, and by the way, here are some ways of doing that!" I realize that the preceding quote is not scientific and I certainly cannot support the statement with hard data, however, I truly believe it to be accurate.

Gabby's students were currently working on projects that were intended to express the students' feelings toward their world and its future. Other than what they had already learned in class with regard to self-expression through art, there seemed to be very little restrictions on creativity but it appeared that all were cutting up old magazines and organizing the pieces into a collage. I walked by one student who was creating a beautiful image of an iceberg floating in shimmering water with a brilliant blue sky for a background. On the iceberg appeared a silhouette of a wind turbine, the same device that is used to produce renewable energy from the wind. The rays from the shining sun seemed to sing out from behind the device. Below was another silhouette of a polar bear with its two cubs raising their heads toward the sun. As I bent over the work, I was stunned to see that every scrap of paper, no matter how small, was shaped like a blade of a wind turbine. I cannot describe exactly how or why but I was overwhelmed with emotion. The student did not even explain the work to me but her art seemed to speak thousands of words and did a much better job than I could ever have done in regard to the urgency by which we need to transition to renewable energy resources.

As I continued to walk through the room, a very interesting project caught my eye. From a few feet away, the picture seemed to be of a tree with a smoke-filled sky above the leaves and a clear blue sky below. A trash-laden stream flowed toward the base of the tree, disappeared into the roots, and emerged in glistening fashion afterwards. Examining the collage closely, I could discern that the entire tree was made of small pictures of people. Conversely, the polluted scenes were made of small pictures of trash, while the healthy environment created from images of natural beauty. As I took the moment in, I had to wonder if what I just experienced could have been translated into a scientific text. As I continued to watch the young man work, I concluded that although a skilled scientist would be able to describe the image before me in great detail, the essence of the work would be lost. There is truly something about the marriage of art and science that must be appreciated if we are to move forward toward a sustainable world.

As I continued to move about the class it was apparent that Gabby had done an outstanding job of infusing the fundamental environmental concepts into her instruction. Not only were the projects powerful forms of expression, they were to be given academic merit as they demonstrated accuracy in their application of scientific principles. One final project that I would like to describe involved an image of a man attempting to cross a rope bridge in what appeared to be a rainforest ecosystem. The bridge was bending from the weight of the man and his belongings, and somehow the student artistically captured the feeling that the bridge was about to give way. It seemed imminent that the man would fall into the raging water below. The man was carrying a sack of jewels on his back. Looking closely, one could see that the jewel shaped pieces were made from pictures of items that typically represent societal wealth such as cars, computers, cellular phones and other consumer goods. "Wow, that is a powerful statement you are making. You make this look so easy," I said. He responded, "Saying what or how I feel is sometimes hard for me, but by using art, everything seems to come out smoothly." I told him, "All I know is that I am certainly impressed. Anyone who knows me understands that I have a hard time drawing stick figures." The student smiled and said, "We all have our strengths, but even stick figures can make a point."

Through her students, Gabby was certainly proving her worth as an ambassador for sustainability. She had taken it upon herself to become eco-literate. She is an artist that does not profess to be an environmental scientist but rather a person who appreciates the sciences. Similarly, I am a scientist that does not profess to be an artist but rather a person who appreciates the arts. We had an interesting discussion about our backgrounds and how far that each of us has come to appreciate the other's natural talents. We came to the conclusion that we were just very happy to be working toward the same goal. My colleagues and I left Gabby's classroom feeling like we just gained a powerful ally in the fight to promote global sustainability.

◆◆◆

As a former department supervisor, I remember the annual struggle associated with procuring funding for our school's art teachers and their students. Every year there seemed to be less and less money available for equipment, activities, and supplies and the arts always seemed to be last on the priority list. I'm confident that many art teachers across the country have shared in this experience. I often wondered if school leadership considered the arts expendable because they felt that these disciplines were not able to contribute in the same utilitarian manner as say, mathematics or science. Regardless, I remember something that one of my mentors had told me when it came to asking for additional funds when others may not yet realize your worth. He professed,

"Never tell them what you did not accomplish because you needed more. Instead, show them what you can accomplish with less and they will certainly provide you with more." Paul, a high school art teacher, demonstrated the wisdom of that statement and put it to use in his classroom.

Paul said to his class, "Let's use our artistic skills to make the world a better place while making some money in the process. We are going to show everyone how to take nothing and make it into something!" The students appeared interested by his statement. He added, "I'll bet that most of you never thought that art can make a positive impact in a utilitarian manner." "What do you mean by utilitarian?" asked one student. Paul responded, "It means applying art to deliver a product or service that people actually need and will pay for. Let me give you an example of a successful business that has turned waste materials into art."

Paul pulled up the website for a company that has recovered millions of pounds of trash from the oceans and coastlines and artistically creates bracelets that are sold for profit. The class enjoyed browsing the company's products that were available for on-line purchase. The students then read about the company founders that went on a surf trip and were devastated by the amount of plastic they found in the ocean. These men could not understand why no one was doing anything about the problem. They did a little research and eventually concluded that the local people did not have the resources to organize or fund a clean up project and needed to concentrate on fishing to feed their families. The class learned about how these young entrepreneurs took it upon themselves to tackle the problem. "These guys are like heroes," said one student. "Yeah, but making jewelry sounds fun and the fact that they are doing something positive is a bonus," said another. "What do you think about the fact that they are able to turn a profit doing something they love while making the world a better place?" asked Paul. The class acknowledged that they were accomplishing something wonderful (Kart, J., 2018).

"Wait, did you hear about those guys that are collecting the oxygen tanks that are left on mountains and using them to make jewelry?" asked a student. Paul had the student look the concept up and display the results on the touchscreen. "Here it is," said the student (https://lokai.com/pages/sherpa-story). "They collect the discarded oxygen tanks from people that climb Mount Everest and instead of just leaving them there as litter, they melt the tanks down, make jewelry, and sell it." Another student was already on his smartphone reading about a couple of entrepreneurs that were making products out of old billboard signs. "Great," said Paul, "You are starting to see that art can be much more than just something to look at."

"Now, what would you say if there were artists that team up with scientists to create works of art that serve a needed purpose?" asked Paul. The faces of the students expressed a sincere interest. Paul displayed an artistic work on the touchscreen. The piece consisted of large, colorful balls floating in a small pond surrounded by a green field of grazing animals. The artwork created an interesting and aesthetically pleasing scene. Once the students had an opportunity to view the image, Paul explained that the balls were actually portable biogas units. The students were amazed to learn that one such unit is capable of providing the average sized poverty stricken family enough energy to cook and illuminate their home using the organic waste provided by two cattle (https://www.superflex.net/tools/supergas). I had to smile as the students expressed their shock.

Paul then showed the class an image of what appeared to be a beautiful garden. This peaceful scene provided a respite from its urban location, a sanctuary within which anyone would enjoy spending some time. The garden, however, was designed to provide food for a soup kitchen. It also allows for homeless individuals to use the garden to cultivate their own produce and become more self-reliant members of society. The class went silent.

Paul then described the Land Art Generator Initiative (LAGI) that brings together science and art in efforts to develop utilitarian works that benefit society (https://landartgenerator.org/). The first work he displayed was called, "Windstock." This enormous and dynamic sculpture resembled a multitude of 50-foot tall blades of grass swaying in the wind. Its resin "poles" are capable of harnessing the wind energy and converting that kinetic motion into useable electricity. Paul told the class that this artwork has an annual capacity of 20,000 megawatt hours. He added that the average American family uses about 10 megawatt hours per year so the amount of electricity generated by this artwork is quite significant.

Paul then put a picture of a work called "Solar Sound Field" on the touchscreen. The students were obviously impressed to learn that as the hot air rose within these tall chimney-like structures energy was produced along with musical notes. They were equally impressed with an artwork known as "Solar Hour Glass" that resembles two huge square sheets bent into the shape of an hourglass. The sheets are made of reflective material that harness and concentrate the reflected sunlight, create steam, and eventually produce electricity. The Solar Hour Glass has an annual energy capacity of 6,000 megawatt hours, demonstrating that in addition to being aesthetically pleasing it serves also as a legitimate renewable energy source.

Paul said, "I can see that many of you are becoming captivated by these concepts. Just so you are aware, these are not my ideas. In fact, much of what I am explaining to you is what I had learned from Mr. Kev Nemelka's Tedtalk on the subject. Paul recounted that Mr. Nemelka said, "If you express your creativity with sustainability and altruism in mind, you can help make the world a better place." Paul said that one of the best ideas he took away from the presentation was the vision that art needs to be held "pragmatically accountable" and can work along with science to make a sustainable future a real possibility (https://kevnemelka.com/filter/rn/T-E-D-x).

"Now it's your turn," said Paul. Paul then organized his students into groups and challenged them to come up with an idea that the class could put into action right here at the high school. The project objective was to reclaim waste material and turn it into something useful that could be sold for a profit. Paul said, "Of course, everything we earn will be given to charity." Paul gave the students the remainder of the period to discuss their ideas and instructed them to be ready the next day with their best utilitarian art concept.

Although I was not able to attend the presentation session, Paul shared that the students conjured up some very creative project ideas. The one that the class voted to pursue they called "Unburied Treasure." This fundraising project involved his art students recovering and utilizing material reclaimed from every waste stream available in the school. From this material, students created custom designed artwork that would be delivered to recipients at the request of others who had made a donation to the project. Paul said that the artwork ranged from small figurines to ornate decorations. The month-long effort resulted in nearly 137 custom projects netting a total profit of $685. The students decided to donate the money to a local youth charity. It proved to be an effective marketing strategy since, along with receiving a unique gift, most people liked knowing that the effort was helping out a worthy cause.

I asked Paul how much instructional time was lost due to the project. His answer really caught me by surprise. "We didn't lose one minute. The kids were so motivated that all work dedicated directly to the project was completed outside of class. The students actually formed their own club and call themselves the *Wasted Artists*." I then asked if the project was worth the effort. He laughed and said, "It didn't cost the art budget one cent in supplies. In fact, I'd say it was worth at least $685." It's good to see that entrepreneurial spirit is alive and well.

Marley teaches elementary school art for her district. I wish I had a video of her facial expressions while we were covering environmental toxicity in one of our presentations. They were nothing less than hysterical! We were discussing how toxins enter the body when Marley said, "My kids are experts at this." Referring to the four "Routes of Entry" displayed on the board, she methodically pointed to each saying, "They will sniff, taste, and touch anything, and if it's pointy, they'll find a way to get poked. Accident prevention is like a second job for an art teacher." Marley was an active participant in what turned into a very productive discussion on environmental toxicity. The group dialogue focused on inhalation, ingestion, skin absorption, and injection as the participants made connections to their own experiences in and out of the classroom.

After returning to her school, Marley did a little research and found that although many of the supplies that she was using claimed to be non-toxic, several still had disclaimers and warnings that made her less comfortable about exposing her students to them. She discovered that some of these "non-toxic" supplies actually contained potential carcinogens. She found that many of these chemicals act as preservatives while others serve to improve the quality of the product. As a result, Marley decided to look into natural alternatives. She realized that she could not replace all of the traditional art supplies but she was prepared to do what she could.

Marley reported that she discovered many natural art materials made from plants and fruits that not only provide an abundance of brilliant colors but also smell good. She experimented with some of these natural supplies and the kids loved them. She said that one of her students told her that the paint he was using smelled "really delicious." I laughed at that since I was the kid that sniffed the markers as soon as the teacher handed them out.

Marley also uncovered a group of these natural products referred to as botanical paints. They are made from fruits, flowers, vegetables, and spices. These completely organic products are water-soluble and biodegradable so using them causes no environmental degradation. She seemed to also like the fact that they come in powder form so she was able to add water to make as much or as little as the students needed. She told us she was also looking into incorporating some projects using natural stains that are made from vegetable juices.

Marley invited us to visit one of her classes in which the students were currently using these natural supplies. She warned us, however, to expect a little more than the average elementary school art class. When the students arrived to class Marley said, "Today we have some visitors." She introduced us to the students and said, "These people are sustainability scientists. They are here to see what we are doing to keep ourselves and the planet healthy." Marley proudly asked if anyone would be willing to explain what is so special about the supplies that are being used for today's project. Without hesitation it seemed like every hand went up. Marley selected a boy that said, "They are healthy for us and the planet." Another student explained how their teacher had told them that bad chemicals called toxins can get into our bodies through our skin, lungs, mouth, or if we get stuck with something like a pen or wire. I shot Marley a smile and said, "Wow, someone has been teaching environmental science in art class." Marley then asked the class if anyone could explain why art and science sometimes have the same goal? A girl raised her hand and said, "Art is making beautiful things and science is trying to keep things beautiful." As a scientist, I truly enjoyed hearing that from today's youth.

Marley provided a few directions as the students retrieved their projects and supplies and got to work. "We are one hundred percent green today but it looks like a typical art class, doesn't it?" asked Marley. I really could not tell any difference. Watching the students, one could see that they had no issues with the natural supplies. In fact, when I asked a student what she thought about the materials she was using, she held up her paintbrush to me and said, "Smell this." I took a sniff and had to say, "It smells like your picture." She smiled. She was painting a scene that included several varieties of fruit.

I thanked Marley and congratulated her on providing a magnificent example of infusing environmental concepts into the instruction. I explained that while many teachers expose their students to concepts pertaining to the field of sustainability, she made these ideas tangible and an immediately relevant part of the physical learning experience. At that moment, the student that was painting the picture of the fruit looked up at me and said, "The good part is that you can smell all you want, and use all you want, there are no chemicals that can harm you or the Earth." I know they say that a picture is worth a thousand words but, in this case, that student's words were worth a thousand pictures.

Sherry is an orchestra teacher who has become quite passionate about the need for developing eco-literate citizens. For several years she has been educating herself in the field of environmental science and sustainability and has provided her students with many interesting and inspirational projects allowing them to express their own views on the topic. "I find that in general, students are disappointed with the way our society is handling the issue of sustainability," said Sherry. She added, "For the most part, I've noticed that young people are less likely than their older counterparts to be misled by unscrupulous individuals that bend the truth in order to gain support for their own personal or political advantage. If teachers in all grade levels and disciplines take it upon themselves to educate their students in sustainability, eventually our society will be capable of making better decisions when it comes to its own future."

I had the privilege of witnessing the end result of one of Sherry's sustainability-themed projects. It was a night that many will never forget. However, there was much work that needed to be accomplished in preparation for that performance. To begin, Sherry asked the students to research examples of what she called, "Triumph and Tragedy" as they related to the health of our species and our planet. In addition to providing a brief account of their triumph or tragedy story to the class, each student was also required to provide a single picture that they felt represented their message and a musical piece that best captured its emotional tone.

Each student was provided the opportunity to describe his/her "triumph" or "tragedy" to the class. As the students spoke, their representative pictures were projected on a screen while their selected music played in the background. After her students completed the first several presentations, Sherry asked the class audience to comment on their overall impressions. One student told her that he never heard such energetic presentations in school before. She was able to ascertain that this seemed to be the consensus of the class. She asked the students to reflect on what may have made these presentations so different from what they were accustomed to. One student offered that music was used to tell part of the story and that aspect is not common in typical school reports. Sherry already knew what the young man meant, but in order to reinforce his statement, she asked him to explain how music "told" part of the story. The student clarified by saying that the music added another dimension to the presentation. He called it, "A dimension of feeling and emotion." Sherry told us that the class seemed to be in complete agreement on this.

Sherry felt that the presentations were a huge success. Her students demonstrated the ability to combine music and science to create emotional yet fact-based statements that expressed their individual and collective environmental viewpoints. However, Sherry was not done. A school musical performance was scheduled for March and Sherry was determined to put the issues, concerns, and success stories that impassioned her students, front and center. She told the class that they would be opening up the performance with a special number called, "Tragedy and Triumph – A Plea for Sustainability."

Sherry admitted that when she first came up with the idea, she was concerned that she might not be able to pull everything off. However, the student motivation was incredible. She said that even she had underestimated the passion and drive the students had when it came to preserving our world and their faith in their own abilities to make a difference. She had helped them realize the influence that music can have on our lives and the decisions that we make, and now they were ready to assume the leading role. The class worked for weeks selecting and practicing the score that would accompany the slide presentation that they themselves compiled.

On the night of the performance, I asked Sherry if she was nervous. "Not at all," she said gesturing toward the orchestra pit. "Just like the fate of the planet, it's now in their hands. They will be fine." That turned out to be quite the understatement. As her orchestra played emotionally charged music, over one hundred images of beauty and degradation were interwoven on a large projection screen. No words were necessary as the visual and acoustical energy filled the auditorium painting accurate and precise accounts of triumphs and tragedies facing our world. Wondrous visions of wildlife were set in opposition to images of ecosystem destruction. Gorgeous vistas and sunsets merged into scenes of political unrest, polluted air, water, and ground. The performance opening brought tears of both sadness and joy to the audience of the packed auditorium. When the orchestra concluded the opening number, the deafening silence soon turned into a thunderous standing ovation!

It was truly a memorable evening. Yes, the orchestra students had delivered an outstanding musical performance but more importantly, their passion and optimism for the future seemed to lift everyone in that audience to a new level. Their ideas, dreams, passions, and internal music were released with brilliance and amplitude and received with appreciation and understanding. Even if only for one night, that young group of future leaders proved to the world what can be done when talent and effort are put toward an achievable goal. Sherry's love for our planet and hope for the future was passed on to her students. They, in turn, used their knowledge and musical talent to inspire others who may possibly do the same.

I was left speechless by what I had just experienced. For years it has been my dream to assist teachers in discovering ways to instill this kind of passion in their students. When I saw Sherry later that evening, I reminded her of what she had told me a few months earlier when she said, "If teachers in all grade levels and disciplines take it upon themselves to educate their students in sustainability, eventually our society will be capable of making better decisions when it comes to its own future." I took her hand and looked in her eyes and said, "Look what you did, . . . Just look what you did." I had to fight back a tear. She could not.

◆◆◆

Several years ago, Michelle developed and piloted a course in fashion design for her district's art department. It has since become a very popular class and she now handles several sections and levels. Teaching fashion design is now her primary focus and Michelle works extremely hard to keep pace with the current trends and adjusts her curriculum to adapt to the changing industry. Michelle brought a very important component to our sustainability workshop when she described a project that she has worked on for the past several years. She refers to the unit as "An Introduction to Upcycling." Basically, she requires her students to take something that has little or no value and transform that into some form of valuable fashion apparel or accessory.

One of the topics we cover in our introductory workshop, known as Integrated Waste Management (IWM), examines the efficiency of production processes. Also known as pollution prevention, IWM employs techniques and strategies designed to reduce resource consumption and waste production while improving profitability. Methods include, but are not limited to, recycling waste back into the production process, finding secondary purposes or buyers for unavoidable by-products, reclaiming or selling otherwise wasted energy, and substituting for the most effectively processed raw materials (What a Waste: An Updated Look into the Future of Solid Waste Management, 2018).

As soon as she heard of IWM at our training session, Michelle identified a potential infusion point for environmental education into her curriculum. She saw a direct connection between IWM and her unit on upcycling and decided to add a new component to her introductory lessons. When she asked us, we were more than happy to provide her with the presentation materials she needed for her class and examples of highly recognized, global corporations that save millions of dollars every year by making IWM a standard practice at their production facilities. Michelle spent an entire lesson introducing IWM to her class. She wanted them to understand that even large companies that are driven by profit see the value in sustainable operations.

When the lesson was completed, she asked the class what integrated waste management has to do with fashion design. One student offered that fashion is a production process too, and he was sure there is a lot of waste that can be recycled, reused, or sold for other purposes. Michelle complimented him on a fine response and told the class that someday they may find themselves working as sustainability professionals in the industry. She said that she certainly encouraged them to do so if that was their dream. Michelle explained, however, that their upcoming unit was on upcycling and since it is a microcosm of the IWM process, she was hoping that learning about its relevance would serve as motivation. The class nodded in agreement.

Michelle distributed a handout that defined the guidelines for the next class project and included a list of examples that had been completed by former students. After the students had some time to read the handout, Michelle shared the story of how she had learned of the ways IWM was being applied in the real world, and that she was amazed by the similarities between what was going on at large corporations and the project that they were about to undertake. She reminded the students that creativity and ingenuity were their best allies and added, "It never hurts to save money, so why not do that and help save the planet while you're at it?"

Months later, Michelle was kind enough to come in and share several of her students' finished projects at one of our introductory seminars. The first items were handbags made of recycled plastic straws. The products were colorful, well-constructed, and certainly utilitarian. Almost everyone agreed that such an accessory was worth at least $50. However, what made this item so special was that unless you looked closely, you would never have known that the raw materials used were recycled plastic straws. "Don't worry," said Michelle, "All of the waste used for these projects has been properly sanitized." Many of the workshop participants laughed as Michelle added, "I know that some of you were wondering."

Michelle then showcased several dresses that were made from fabrics that had been recovered solely from the school's waste stream. Although I am no fashion guru, the dresses appeared to be well designed and trendy. She asked, "Can any of you tell that these were made from materials that would have otherwise been headed to the landfill?" That's when you had to admit that these students were really doing something remarkable.

"What do you think about these?" Michelle said as she placed what seemed to be floppy beach hats on the people in the first few rows. "Other than the inner liner, the entire item is made from recycled plastic," added

Michelle. From a short distance, the hats looked like common shade hats donning flowers and decorative add-ons. Looking closely, however, one discovered that these items were once parts of colored bottles, six-pack holders, product containers, and all other kinds of plastic items. Not only were the hats functional and comfortable, they were fun and interesting to look at. Michelle twisted one of the hats to demonstrate the fact that the students went to great lengths to make their products durable. Michelle then took a bottle of water and poured it on the top of one of the hats. They are also waterproof!

"If any of you are wrestling coaches you may enjoy this next one," said Michelle as she took off her shoes and slipped on a pair of flip-flops. "Ha! Those are made out of old wrestling mats, aren't they?" said one of our physical education participants. "You got it," said Michelle pointing to the coach. She explained that after several of the students custom-made them for the school's wrestlers, they started getting orders for more but ran out of mat. The shoes looked very professional, had no rough edges, and of course, included recycled and colorfully dyed laces.

Michelle then presented a myriad of other fashionable items and accessories made from all types of discarded materials. It was hard to believe that almost everything we were looking at was once destined for the dump. "Have any of the students thought about going into business with these ideas?" asked one of the workshop attendees. Michelle told us that many of the students have dreams of being entrepreneurs but as of yet, her class has failed to produce any millionaires. She did tell us that she has spoken to the school's business teacher about a future interdisciplinary project toward that end.

I was very happy that Michelle had come in to share her students' work with us but I was also very appreciative of the fact that she was able to communicate to our attendees that promoting eco-literacy is everyone's job. She explained that when she first signed up for our sustainability training, she did not see the immediate connection to fashion. Michelle added, "It's probably like that for most teachers, however, I'd bet that once an educator becomes eco-literate, as I have, they will not only be able, but they will also want to relate these important environmental issues to their curricula. The students love it and it is truly a worthwhile effort."

It is no secret that songwriters have had a strong influence on the generational movements of the past. I remember many of the songs that my older sister would listen to on the radio. Her generation's music clearly discouraged war and violence and promoted peace and love. Although I never really thought of it before meeting a music teacher by the name of Charlie, I suddenly realized that in high school many of the songs that I listened to encouraged individual success, and much emphasis was placed on materialistic possessions. In fact, I can't get a song about a materialistic girl from the 80s out of my head as I'm writing this sentence. Charlie, on the other hand, has always understood the correlation between popular music and the values, dreams, and needs of the young people who listen to it. Although there are many different issues facing today's youth that find their way into pop culture, the issue of sustainability is becoming more and more prevalent.

Charlie provided his class with a brief overview of the current major environmental issues. He introduced his students to the problems associated with resource depletion, environmental degradation, overpopulation, climate change, and pollution. It soon became apparent that these concepts were not foreign to his students. They were already well aware of their existence and many expressed a feeling of anger that they were the generation that needed to "fix" these problems. Charlie had the touchscreen all ready to go with a song that he had found while researching sustainability. It was a rap song entitled, "Sustainable Development Goals: Improve Life All Around the Globe" (United Nations, 2017).

I was certainly aware of the United Nation's Sustainable Development Goals but I had no idea that there was a song about them. It was an extra treat that Charlie sang the entire lyrics along with the music. The kids loved it and they went crazy! Charlie explained that he had chosen to play this song for his students because it represents all of the key concepts that people around the world should be trying to live by. He said that the artist is attempting to educate everyone, especially young people about important issues such as clean air and water and all of the things that we need to do in order to protect the planet and everything that lives on it (About the Sustainable Development Goals - United Nations Sustainable Development, 2015).

Charlie looked at me and said, "Watch what music can do." I didn't understand exactly what he meant at first.

"Do you think the message got through?" he asked me and then said to the class, "Let's see how many of the sustainability goals we can remember." I must say that I was astonished by what I witnessed. One by one, the actual goals rolled in as the class listed climate action, education, zero hunger, no poverty, clean water, etc. In fact, the class was able to recall 14 of the 17 goals after only one run through! Back when I was teaching chemistry, I often had difficulty getting my students to remember the first several elements of the periodic table after a whole week of study, let alone one reading. How the heck did they do that? I thought for a moment and then I remembered Charlie saying, "Watch what music can do." I recalled how adept my friends and I were at learning the lyrics to the songs that we grew up with and I understood what he meant. Music certainly has an influence on people, and in this case, a very positive one.

When his presentation was over Charlie said, "I am going to give you a few minutes to reflect on this. Think of a song that you have heard in your life that deals with one or more of the environmental issues that we have just discussed." After several minutes, Charlie said, "Raise your hand if you were able to think of a song right off the top of your head that addresses the concept of sustainability." Every hand went up.

Charlie then explained the homework assignment to the class that was displayed on the touchscreen. "Find a song that in some way addresses the issue of sustainability. The song does not have to be recent, but must reflect the environmental problems that, unfortunately, people of your generation will need to address." Charlie added, "The reason I say that the song need not be recent is that my generation has known about these issues for decades. We have failed to address these problems and now future generations will inherit our burden. On behalf of all of the baby boomers out there, please accept my apologies." The class let out a half-hearted laugh as one student said, "Hey, at least you admit it." Charlie smiled and said, "Please be prepared to explain why you chose the song that you did and the message that you believe the artist is attempting to make." As the bell rang, it was obvious that the students were motivated by the assignment. The singing gave it away.

The next day afforded the students their turn to share some of their favorite songs that promote eco-literacy, encourage sustainability, or address environmental issues. The first student to present introduced what she believed to be a brand-new song since both she and her peers all seemed to know the lyrics by heart. I laughed silently because when I heard the first remake of that song, I thought it was brand new then! The truth is that the original song first made the scene back in the 70s. I guess there is a moral in that short history lesson which is that great songs never die, they just get passed on from one generation to the next.

The student said that she was saddened by the song's premise that sometimes we change our environment in an attempt to make it better. However, what we end up finding out is that the Earth was really better off just the way it was. The student explained that she felt the artist was trying to point out, "The world is perfect just the way it is and people have created an artificial society that will never be able to surpass or even equal nature's beauty." When I heard that statement made by this impressionable young person, I couldn't help but wonder if the song's writer would ever have dreamed of the positive impact that it would have on so many people throughout the years.

The next student to present started her video and said, "The song I have chosen is about the Earth telling us that we are running out of time. However, if we embrace truth, and if everyone comes together to make a positive change we can survive. On the other hand, if we stay the path that we are on, both we and our planet will suffer." The video's initial images were both dark and overwhelmingly depressing. However, the tone seemed to gradually change as more and more uplifting scenes reflected a much lighter, positive, and optimistic mood. "I want to be part of that future, a good and sustainable future. I want to help make it that way," said the young lady as she held back a tear. The class was silent.

I really enjoyed watching the faces of the students while the final song of the day played. It appeared that the students recognized the artist's message in a manner similar to how I could see the "light bulbs" going off in my students' heads. The student explained how he believed certain scenes symbolized progress and the incredible achievements of mankind that falsely give us a sense that we are in control of our destiny. However, he also explained that he felt the artists flashed in scenes of a beautiful sky and a young couple in love because they wanted to warn us that we needed to cherish and protect what is truly a beautiful world. The student said that the song's message is simple, "We have a good thing going but we are in danger of losing it. Every day is a gift and so is our world. As a species, we are not as entitled as we sometimes believe ourselves to be. We must accept our place in the world and take responsibility for sustaining the planet."

"I've heard my students listening to that song over a hundred times and I never realized what it was all about. Now that you have explained it, I understand it; it makes sense to me," said a veteran teacher that happened to be passing by and stopped in to see what was going on. She was obviously a well-respected and popular teacher and the students appeared very comfortable giving her looks as if she was from another planet. "Hey, that song is not from my generation," she said in her defense. Charlie turned to the teacher and said, "The music of every generation is unique. I believe that the future belongs to the people that are able to understand the music of the day. With that ability comes the responsibility to make the world a better place. Hopefully, generations to follow will listen only to songs of a sustainable future."

The bell was about to ring so Charlie told the class they would continue the next time that they met. When the class was over, I thanked Charlie and told him that he really demonstrated the power that music has in our lives. He reminded me that songs play constantly in our heads and it is why advertisers use catchy jingles. As I left Charlie's school that day, I started thinking about wars that had ended, positive political decisions that were made, and international agreements that had been achieved throughout history. I wondered, what songs were playing at those times? I'll bet you have made a decision or two based on the last song that you had heard. I know I have.

Mark brought sustainability education into his woodshop class by laying out some basic facts for his students and allowing them an opportunity to put their woodworking and creative skills to task. In short, he identified a big problem facing our world and gave them a chance to be part of the solution. Mark said, "Not all wood is created equal. Some trees take far too long to mature to make them a sustainable option." He added that using these trees can lead to human rights abuses, threats to endangered species, habitat loss, and obviously resource depletion (What is Sustainable Forestry, 2016).

The class learned that softwood trees such as pine are a good choice because they are fast growing and easily replaced. Hardwoods such as oak, on the other hand, take much longer to grow so a greater time investment is required. Soft or hardwood, as long as the trees can be replaced at the same rate as they are removed, we can consider the practice sustainable. However, Mark explained that much of the time, trees are harvested too rapidly.

Mark then showed a brief documentary on deforestation. The film presented quantitative data on the depletion of this resource in a particular area and the effects on surrounding ecosystems. One student asked, "Couldn't the people who live there see what was happening? I mean, there had to be a point at which the people realized they were in big trouble when almost all of their trees were gone." Before Mark could reply, another student said, "Maybe they knew they were screwed but since they relied on the wood for their jobs, they had no choice." Mark interjected, "That's a good point. Maybe it was too late for the people living in that region, but it's certainly not too late for us and we are going to do our part to get the word out." The class was attentively listening.

Mark said, "Our next project will involve the use of one of two sustainable wood resources, bamboo and reclaimed wood." Mark explained that bamboo is very light and strong and grows quickly in many environments. The resource can be harvested in only three to five years. In addition, bamboo is said to have antibacterial qualities, is eco-friendly, and multi-functional. Mark described reclaimed wood as being just what it sounds like. He said, "Any wood that is about to be thrown away that can be reused for another purpose is considered reclaimed wood. If someone already made the mistake of using a poor choice of wood in the first place, the least we can do is extend the usefulness of that material." Mark then set the guidelines for the upcoming project, challenging the students to use either bamboo or reclaimed wood and put that resource to use in a way to promote sustainable living. "So, you will be part of the solution in two ways," said Mark. "First, you will be demonstrating that you are eco-conscious by using a sustainable resource. Second, your project will, in some way, promote sustainable practices in others."

Mark shared some of the completed projects at one of our introductory workshops. One young man created a paper towel dispenser made of bamboo. This professional-looking item proudly displayed the inscription, *Made From 100% Sustainable Materials.* On the base of the dispenser, an inscription read, *Are you sure that you need one?* The second project Mark showed us was a set of wooden dishes, also made from bamboo. Each dish was stamped with the saying, *Grown Not Thrown.* This was an interesting contrast to disposable paper or plastic plates. A third item made from bamboo was a planter with the inscription, *Use me wisely, I was wisely used.* One of our workshop attendees asked if one could be made for her. She thought it would be perfect for growing a Christmas tree that could be used year after year.

Mark then showed us a sharp-looking recycling bin. What made this project so unique was that the piece was constructed using recycled materials. The student included a very impressive "Certificate of Authenticity" that certified the bin was indeed made from discarded refuse. When someone else has gone to such great lengths to provide you with a receptacle created from reclaimed items, it's plainly irresponsible to not recycle. A second project made from reclaimed wood was a beautifully crafted coffee table. Other than the inscription that read, *Made from Reclaimed Shipping Pallets*, there was no way anyone would have guessed that the wood used to make this perfectly finished table was on its way to the landfill.

The last piece Mark shared with us was truly remarkable. One of his students rooted through a dumpster of a house that was being remodeled. Using nothing but what he found, he created an intricately designed cabinet. Had I seen this piece in a high-end furniture store with a one-thousand-dollar price tag, I would never have thought of questioning its value.

Mark said his students really enjoyed this project because they felt that they were doing something beyond just improving their woodworking skills and building some cool stuff, they were also making a statement. Mark said he was surprised by how well his students responded to this challenge. He was nervous that they might blow it off as some kind of "nerdy" project. Instead, as one of his students put it, "It was great to have a chance to create something that will make a difference in another person's life. If everyone does that, we can make a difference in the world."

Paula teaches several levels of theater for her school. After attending one of our seminars she asked if she could borrow a set of *Sustainable Education* books for her students. She said that she had a great idea on how she could infuse environmental education immediately into her instruction. She began the project with a very general introduction to the major issues discussed in the book. She then organized her class into four groups. She instructed each team to select one environmental issue and create a short skit that could be performed on stage in order to raise environmental awareness of the topic. She added that the topics were on a first come first serve basis so as soon as the group selected an issue, they were to notify her.

"It's always fun to watch the students when they are creating something on their own but this was extra special because they seemed to be on a mission," said Paula. The students knew that in order to develop an accurate presentation, they first had to become experts in their respective topics. Although all of the groups used *Sustainable Education* to gain a fundamental introduction, most conducted additional outside research using a variety of sources. "They really seemed to want to get everything right," said Paula.

The next stage was the script development. Paula noted that the teams created characters that fit the theatrical skill sets of the actors that would be performing the skits. When done, the teams performed dry runs before the dress rehearsals. Finally, it was show time and we were very appreciative that Paula invited us to the actual performances.

The first group to perform selected the topic of water treatment. The skit was entitled, "Skipper's Big Adventure." The skit told the tale of Skipper the goldfish's travels after his owner mistakenly flushed him down the toilet. The group created a hilarious and technically accurate story of Skipper as he encountered all of the different mechanisms and processes involved in wastewater treatment. It was obvious that the students were having a blast and so were members of the audience. Eventually, Skipper made it through the wastewater treatment facility, into a stream, and found a new home in a beautiful and healthy lake. I may not be a thespian but I can certainly say that it was a lot of fun and very educational for all who were watching.

The second group's presentation started out on a sad note but soon took a positive turn. It was a story of a polar bear cub that was separated from its family. He had wandered off and by the time he returned, the ice sheet between he and his home had melted. We learn later in the skit that this wasn't supposed to happen but because of human induced climate change, the normal thawing patterns had been disrupted. Sadly, because there was not enough ice to support her during her difficult rescue attempt, the cub's mother drowned in an effort to reach her cub. This powerful story really made you feel for the plight of the polar bear. What was very interesting was that this skit contained a sub plot of an ambitious politician, completely disconnected from nature, unwilling to accept the reality of climate change and unsympathetic to the tragedy unfolding before us. Without identifying the individuals by name or stating that actual quotes were being used, anyone who is up on current politics knew that the team had done their research. The audience cheered when at the end of the skit, the antagonistic politician was voted out of office and the polar bear cub finally made it home.

Team three created a skit that started off very slowly, literally and figuratively. They used paper dolls as props that needed to be fed. After the dolls were fed, they multiplied and again needed to be fed. After they were fed they multiplied and so on. While the audience was watching this amplifying feedback loop occur time and time again, the group members were methodically speaking the words, "Gotta be fed; gotta make food; gotta think hard; whew, we made it." These phrases that started off slowly along with the multiplication process soon accelerated to a fevered chant. The pace increased and the dolls multiplied until finally the entire process came to a sudden halt. The lights went out and the stage became silent. So did the audience. It was only about 20 seconds but it felt like several minutes had passed before someone finally started applauding and then the entire audience joined in. I'd say that group three got their point across.

The last team's skit was an incredibly humorous story of three aliens that landed on the Earth and then returned to their home world to report what they had observed. The skit was hysterical from the standpoint that any species crazy enough to do what the aliens were recounting would be characterized as mentally insane. Unfortunately, the skit was equally terrifying from the standpoint that we are doing all of the things the aliens were reporting! The aliens spoke of pollution, habitat destruction, and burning of fossil fuels as if these were the means by which this species had chosen to end its own existence. Many of us did not know whether to applaud or hold our heads at the end of that one.

I knew immediately that Paula had accomplished something special with her class. Later that year, as part of the school's Earth Day celebration, the principal arranged an assembly so that the entire student body could benefit from what Paula's class had done. This was the perfect example of students taking ownership of their learning, applying their skills and talents, and creating a meaningful product. If you think about what happened here, you will see how much of an impact one teacher can have. It all started with Paula. This one teacher inspired approximately 20 students to create their own visions of the future and spread their message to over 800 others from their school. I'm sure that many conversations had also taken place later that evening at dinner tables throughout the community. Through the arts, the truth of science can be told, shielded from deception. Powerful indeed are the sustainable arts.

Chapter 11 – Language, A Scientific Tool

In high school, I really enjoyed my English and foreign language classes. I loved reading and discussing Shakespearian plays, the Greek tragedies, and contemporary novels with my peers. Although my annunciation was probably atrocious, I also took pride in learning how to read and write in Spanish and French and later reaped some of the benefits that those skills provided. However, I was one of those students that excelled in science and mathematics so I was forever encouraged by my teachers to continue along that path. In those days, if you showed any promise as a science or math student, you were destined for a career in those fields, end of discussion!

As it turns out, I did end up becoming a scientist but fortunately for me, I never lost my appreciation for spoken and written language. During my freshman year at Rutgers, one of my professors had a saying. He would tell us, "Language is a scientific tool, use it with precision." I never forgot those words and I often repeated them to my students. Language is definitely a scientific tool and we should treat it as such. Without a strong command of language, people cannot properly express themselves, let alone an intricate mathematical or scientific complexity.

My first public school supervisor had another powerful saying. He would tell us, "Remember that you are not teaching your subject, you are teaching your students." I often like to combine these two powerful sayings whenever I am addressing English or foreign language teachers and profess, "Teach your students to use the scientific tool of language with precision so that they may create for themselves a successful future."

The importance of selecting an appropriate subject medium through which the art of reading and writing can be taught and skills mastered should not be underestimated. If you try to think back to your early days of English or foreign language class, you may have actually learned much more than just the curricular standards associated with each particular course. I can certainly recall an experience that I had while taking my SATs, a requirement for the college application process. Whoever developed the reading comprehension section of the test decided to include a selection that painstakingly detailed the process by which raindrops are formed.

I remember reading at least three full pages of text and having to answer only four multiple choice questions pertaining to the process of raindrop formation. "You have to be kidding," I thought to myself. "Why the heck are they wasting my time making me read about raindrops? This was supposed to be about English and reading comprehension. They should be asking me to read some story and recount who did what to whom?" To this day I have no recollection of what my SAT score was, what I was wearing, or even where I took the exam. What I do recall after nearly forty years is the exact process by which raindrops are formed! I'll spare you the details. You can give me a call if you really want to know.

The following lessons and projects are the result of visionary English and foreign language teachers that successfully infused environmental education and concepts associated with sustainability into their instruction. They used these ideas as the medium through which they effectively and efficiently met their original curricular goals.

At SEA, we do not promote any specific sustainability or environmental curriculum, instead we encourage teachers to educate themselves and in turn, pass that knowledge on to their students. It's the old, "teach a man to fish" concept. Sharon is the perfect example of a teacher who has successfully educated herself in the field of environmental science and has now developed into an extremely effective and eco-literate leader.

Sharon is a French teacher and obviously a strong advocate for eco-literacy in the classroom. At one of our recent seminars, she expressed her eagerness to start making environmental education a secondary goal in her classroom. "Why not?" she said, "There is nothing in the State standards that mandates the subject matter that I use to achieve my curricular goals."

When the students entered Sharon's class, they immediately saw a picture of a woman in a driveway who was clearly choosing to use her bicycle instead of the car. Although my French was extremely rusty, I could tell that both she and the students became immediately engaged in a conversation involving the woman in the picture. Sharon was very adept at using facial expression and physical gesture to guide students through the discussion. In order to help me understand what was going on, Sharon instructed the students to translate what they were saying in French into English. What a great use of an available tool . . . the old guy in the back of the room.

Sharon began by asking something very casually in French. One student responded to her and then she gestured toward me. The student turned to me and said, "She asked why we thought the woman was taking the bicycle instead of the car and I thought the woman wanted to get exercise." Another student said, "Maybe she wanted to save gas." Still another offered that perhaps she wanted to do something that was better for the environment. The exercise of translating every sentence for me was obviously hindering the flow of the class dialogue so Sharon apologized in French telling me that I was "slowing the class down." The students and I all laughed. I was more than happy to just sit back and observe anyway.

The class discussed the picture for a few more minutes before Sharon displayed some facts regarding air pollution emissions from motor vehicles on the touchscreen. The data table was obviously in French, however, since the discussion continued, it was apparent that the students were able to understand the material being presented. The next animated slide identified the basic reactions involved when primary pollutants from car exhaust react with water in the air to produce secondary pollutants such as smog and oxides of nitrogen that cause acid rain. I was amazed. Sharon was teaching her students the fundamentals of air pollution in French class. Like she said, "Why not?" They were certainly meeting their curricular goals.

By the time the class was finished, I felt as if I had just participated in an introductory environmental chemistry lesson in Paris! This was truly an outstanding example of infusing environmental education into the classroom. I asked the students what they thought of the lesson. One student said, "We do this all of the time. I like it because while I'm concentrating on an important topic like the air pollution today, I think in French, not English." Another student turned to me and said, "Yeah, that's true. I know that sounds weird but does that make sense to you?" "Yes," I replied, "All the sense in the world." What was so wonderful about this lesson was that Sharon's students knew they were not going to be held accountable for what they had learned about air pollution. So what was their motivation? All too often we find ourselves "teaching to the test" just as our students try to "learn for the test." Isn't it comforting to know that if you choose the right medium, sometimes it's just fun to teach, interesting to learn, and motivation simply takes care of itself?

Lisa's English class had just finished their unit on the Shakespearian play, *King Lear*. Many of these students had also read and discussed other famous works by Shakespeare such as *Macbeth* and *Romeo and Juliet*. Lisa felt that the class could use some time to prepare for their upcoming assessment so she decided to infuse some environmental education and give the class a brief history lesson, discussing a little bit about the life and times of this well-known playwright.

Lisa explained to her class that the average life expectancy in England during Shakespeare's time was only about 35 years, and infant mortality was extremely high. "As terrible as this may sound," said Lisa, "people often gave their children the same first names because they did not expect them all to survive." Lisa described the poor sanitary conditions that included open sewers in the streets and the lack of knowledge that led to the spread of disease, especially when it came to the operation of public water supplies. She told the class there was such a lack of clean water that it was common practice for people to bathe only once a year, or not at all, due to the fear of getting sick. She described how the bubonic plague first struck England between 1592 and 1594. This was a terrible illness causing excruciating pain and victims of the disease were reported leaping from windows in order to avoid this manner of death. In 1603, the plague caused an estimated 30,000 deaths, or one sixth of London's population (Shapiro, J., 2015).

The class appeared mesmerized by what they were hearing. "Where did the bubonic plague come from in the first place?" asked one student. Lisa had done her homework and was able to respond, "Rats were carrying fleas that transmitted the illness." She explained that in scientific terms, the fleas are referred to as the "vector" or the means by which pathogens or disease-causing organisms are introduced to the host. Lisa explained that during the midst of production of some of the best plays ever staged, including *Macbeth* and *King Lear*, all of this suffering was occurring. Unfortunately, the plague had caused a huge strain on the acting community and Shakespeare's company, the Kings Men, closed the Globe Theater.

One student said, "I'm so happy that I live in our time. At least we have everything figured out." Having attended one of our seminars, Lisa was well prepared to handle that naïve comment. She responded, "This is a wonderful time to be alive but we had better make sure that we don't take it for granted and learn how to sustain our society." Lisa then explained how it is our advanced technology that has allowed us to enjoy such long lifespans. However, she also described the exponential growth that our species is experiencing and outlined many of the problems associated with overpopulation. In addition to resource depletion, pollution, and a myriad of other problems, we must remember that disease-causing organisms are always present and without our technology, we remain as vulnerable as the people of Shakespeare's time. "That could never happen again," said one young man.

Lisa expected this reaction from some of her students and said, "Look at it this way. Imagine that you have 10 fish in a 10-gallon aquarium. As long as you feed them and have some sort of oxygen producing and water purifying plant such as elodea in the tank, the fish should be fine. If the fish population doubles, they should still survive as long as you increase the food supply and use electricity to power devices that help the plants filter and aerate the water. You can think of the aerator and filter as representing our technology. Now, imagine that the population doubles again. You now have 40 fish in a 10-gallon tank. Regardless of any plants that may be present, without the aerator or filter, the fish will die. In addition, just think how quickly a disease could wipe out the population in such an overcrowded scenario."

The student smiled and said, "So we just need to keep our filters and aerators running and we all will be fine." "Okay, smarty pants," said Lisa, "but what happens when we run out of the fossil fuels that our society has become so dependent on?" The student smiled and said, "Go Nuclear!" The class laughed but Lisa certainly got her point across. "I'll leave the discussion as to the pros and cons of alternative energy resources to your science teachers. For now, let's just say that we do have it better than Shakespeare and people from his era."

Lisa and her class began discussing how the environmental conditions of Shakespeare's time may have influenced his writing. The students cited scenes from several of his plays that they felt might have been included for these reasons. "We may never know," said Lisa and added, "Scholars often wonder what Shakespeare was doing in the last years of his life. Yes, there is much that we just don't know," she concluded.

The bell was about to ring so Lisa reminded the class to review for tomorrow's assessment. "Will any of the material that we went over today be on the test?" asked a student. "No, do you want it to be?" responded Lisa. The student that Lisa referred to as the "smarty pants" said, "Yes! It's the first stuff that I understood all year." The class laughed; he was quite an amusing character. I'm sure that his statement was simply made in jest, however I could not help but wonder what the impact of Lisa's lesson today might have on some of these students. In fact, I would bet that it is quite possible that every student in Lisa's class will forever remember this lesson. As the students were leaving the classroom, I asked Lisa how much time she spent researching the information that she used. She held up her phone and said, "Ten minutes?" Talk about a good return on your investment!

Roland teaches grade school Spanish for his district. He takes pride in educating students about the Spanish language as well as the cultural aspects of the countries that speak and use that language. Roland realized that his students did not have an appreciation for many of the differences in the cultures, let alone the ecological footprints that exist between citizens of the United States and those of many of the countries that speak the language that they are studying. After participating in one of our introductory workshops, Roland took it upon himself to teach the concept of the IPAT model to his students.

Roland began his lesson by asking, "How many of you have ever walked on newly cut grass?" The majority of students raised their hands. He then selected one of those students and asked her, "What did the grass look like after you stepped on it?" She replied, "I left my footprints." Roland thanked the student for her answer and explained that just like a footprint left on the grass, people and countries leave a "footprint" on the Earth. He equated both types of footprints to damage. In one instance, the damage is to the grass and in the other it is inflicted upon the planet.

"Did you know that some countries have a bigger footprint than others when it comes to damaging the Earth?" Roland asked. A student raised his hand and said, "We have a big footprint here in America because we waste a lot of stuff." Roland asked, "Why do you think we waste so much?" The class was silent and then one girl said, "We have a lot of money so we buy things and then just throw them away. In other countries they don't have as much money so they have to save or recycle whatever they can." Roland was visibly pleased with that answer and defined the term "affluence" for his students. Roland explained that affluence is the amount of money or wealth that a person or country has and said, "Yes, our country is very affluent. The more affluent a country is, the larger its footprint tends to be."

Roland said, "We have learned about the country of Guatemala and their culture in class. What can you tell me about that country's affluence, compared to the United States?" The entire class seemed to immediately respond in unison, "Much lower than us." "You are correct about that," said Roland, "What about their population compared to us?" One student said, "The population is lower too." Roland told the class that so far, they were, "two for two." He added that the lower a country's population, the less its footprint tends to be.

Roland then seemed to change the subject by asking, "How many of you have cell phones?" The class laughed and said together, "All of us," as they held up their phones to show him. "That's fine. You can put them away now. Do you think that every student in Guatemala has a cell phone?" asked Roland. A student replied, "No. Maybe only a few." "How many of you would agree that overall, the United States has more technology than does the country of Guatemala?" Almost every hand went up. Roland explained that the greater a country's technology, the more its impact on the planet tends to be.

Roland then wrote the following equation on the board: *Impact = Population x Affluence x Technology*, or *I = PAT* (Mcnicoll, G., 2015). He said that you can use this equation to find out what person or country has the greater impact, or is causing the greater damage to the planet. Roland explained that based on what the class had just discussed, they should be able to determine whether the United States or Guatemala is causing more environmental damage to the planet. It did not take long for the students to identify the United States as the "winner" in this category since all three factors; population, affluence, and technology were all greater for the United States.

One student asked, "Does this mean that people from the United States are bad?" "That depends on what you mean by bad. What do you think?" asked Roland. The boy replied, "I don't think so. We are lucky and we also help other countries out so that does not make us bad." "That's a fair and acceptable answer in my opinion," said Roland. Another student raised his hand and said, "Since we have such a better lifestyle, people from counties like Guatemala want to come here. That's causing a lot of people to get upset, isn't it?" Roland smiled and said, "Immigration is definitely a topic that is widely debated in our country, however, let's stick to the concept of impact." The class discussion immediately returned to the mathematical simplicity of the IPAT Model. I gave Roland credit for how he handled that student's inquiry. He provided the student with an appropriate answer while discouraging a political discussion that would best be handled later in the student's educational experience.

"Do all Spanish speaking countries have a low impact on the planet?" asked Roland. "Probably not. What about Spain? They have a lot of technology, they are pretty wealthy, and for their size, aren't they kind of populated?" replied a young girl. "Wow, you guys are really understanding how this works. Yes, you are correct but can you still see a difference between Spain and the United States?" asked Roland. The class seemed to ponder the question for a few moments and then a student said, "Spain has been around for much longer than the United States so they have learned to be more sustainable." I thought Roland was going to fall down when he heard that answer. I almost fell off my chair myself. "I have to ask," said Roland, "What do you mean by more sustainable?" The student replied, "Well, sustainability means to keep things going and they must have figured it out by now or things would have fallen apart for them. They've been around for thousands of years, right? The United States has only been around for a few centuries so compared to them; we probably look like a bunch of spoiled kids wasting our money." Roland and I just looked at each other and blinked. "Only from the mouths of babes," I thought. Could anyone have said it better?

Roland wrapped up the lesson with some vocabulary and got the class right back on track so that they would continue to meet all of their curricular goals. He let the students know what they could expect the next time the class met. If my child were taking Spanish, I'd want him or her in Roland's class because it seemed like you get bonus education for free. As a former supervisor charged with performing classroom observations, I realize that the daily grind in some foreign language classes can often lead to inefficiency in content comprehension and retention. By mixing in outside but related information as Roland did here, the students stay focused, motivated, and everything remains fresh. For the record, I have visited Guatemala and toured their schools. I must say that I was more than impressed with the students' appreciation for education, sustainability practices, and determination to make this world a better place. Hopefully, if all teachers do their part, as Roland is doing, we will be able to secure a sustainable future for all of our children.

Tara wanted her students to practice their skills at writing well-constructed essays and she found an effective, motivational, and multi-faceted way for them to do so. She had always known that students enjoyed writing about their career dreams however this time she added a new twist to the age-old standby. Tara required that her students also explain how the concept of sustainability in some way, shape, or form will be part of their potential future career. She explained to the class that she expected their immediate reaction to be similar to how she felt when she was asked to infuse environmental education into her teaching. "At first, I thought that English and environmental science had nothing to do with one another," said Tara. "I'll admit that I believed the whole idea was a waste of time until I started examining the concept of sustainability more closely."

Tara asked the class to bear with her as she felt the need to explain how and why sustainability education has become such an important part of her life. Tara began by providing the class an account of what sustainability means to her. She explained how she views people as stealing so much from the Earth without paying the planet back for what has been taken. She described how people continue to live "The American Dream" with certain expectations, however, common sense tells us that sooner or later our resources will be depleted and that those expectations are unrealistic. "In other words, we are an unsustainable society," said Tara.

She added that her generation has failed to do its part in restoring the environmental degradation that has occurred. "That leaves you guys holding the bag. Your generation will have no choice but to face and deal with very difficult problems that society has ignored in hopes that miraculously, these issues would all just go away. That is unfair and it is why I believe every teacher has the responsibility to provide his or her students with the tools that they will need to create a sustainable future."

Tara confided that years ago she would have never envisioned herself promoting eco-literacy because she had always thought her job was to teach English as it had always been done before and outlined in the district's curricular guide. However, she has now set a more altruistic goal for herself as an English teacher. "Sustainability is everyone's job and my job is to assist all of you in becoming not just more literate but more eco-literate," said Tara. It was obvious that the students were moved and inspired.

Tara paused and said, "I have told you all of this because I want you to understand the importance of the assignment you are about to begin. I could have asked you to simply discuss your career goals but instead, I'm asking you to take it one step further by investigating the concept of sustainability and envisioning how it may apply to your future aspirations. I wanted you to realize that I have found a way to infuse sustainability education into my career. So, you see, I'm not asking you to do anything more than I am requiring of myself." The class nodded in approval.

Tara shared the content of several of the resulting essays at one of our sustainability workshops. One student dreamed of becoming a physician. He spoke in depth of the root causes of disease and the biological and physical hazards that are determined primarily by a person's surrounding environmental conditions. He seemed to handle his essay as well as a practicing physician, perfectly explaining the routes of entry that toxins take as they enter the human body. He noted that in order to sustain our way of living, technology and medicine will have to keep pace with the exponential population growth that our species is experiencing. He also discussed the need for physicians to understand how the body responds to stimuli associated with changing external conditions such as environmental degradation, pollution, climate change, and population increases in urban areas.

Another student dreamed of making a living as a professional athlete and made an immediate connection between sustaining human physical performance and the sustainability of our society. His essay supported his opening statement as he made analogies between proper nutrition and renewable energy resources; the personal sacrifice necessary for transitioning into a well-conditioned athlete and the personal sacrifices necessary for transitioning into a sustainable society; and the rewards associated with becoming a successful athlete and the rewards associated with becoming a sustainable society.

One young woman wished to someday become a mathematics teacher. She described her desire to follow in the footsteps of her high school English teacher who, "Taught us much more than English. She showed us how we can put our personal talents to use to create a better world." The student explained how she hoped that her generation would be successful in transitioning society to one that was truly sustainable and she said that she felt responsible for teaching her students to avoid the mistakes made by previous generations. Tara must have shared our book with her students because this future teacher referred to *Sustainable Education* and appropriately referenced information that supported her case. I really do hope that this student fulfills her dreams of becoming a teacher. If every educator started with a goal like this, our planet would be destined for a brilliant future.

An essay written by a future travel consultant described his ideal career. He wishes to visit different parts of the world and share his experiences with anyone who will listen. He described some of the tragic stories that he has heard about in regard to environmental degradation occurring in some of the most beautiful locations on our planet. Among others, he described vanishing rainforests due to clear-cutting practices and the bleaching of our coral reefs as one of the effects of climate change. He unfortunately wondered if his career goal would even be possible in a world where beautiful and unspoiled locations are becoming less and less common.

One of the essays focused on the career of architectural engineer. The student explained that his father is an engineer and he always wanted to work in the same field as his dad. However, the student had obviously done his research and knew that times were changing and he was going to have to understand and work with the new and improved technologies that were becoming available. He said that in college he would be learning about how the buildings of tomorrow will be expected to meet LEED or US Green Building standards. He described green buildings as structures that included components such as water purification processes, passive and active solar heating and cooling technologies, as well as super-efficient and renewable energy use systems.

Another student aspired to go into business marketing and explained how sustainability is becoming a key component to any successful organization. He described a process referred to as "closed-loop cycling." Applying this system, waste materials are not discarded but rather re-introduced into the manufacturing process of a product. This practice not only saves money and is environmentally sound it also promotes a healthy and positive corporate image. He used the well-known and financially successful company Nike as an example (Larson, A., & York, J., 2017). If every future business leader possessed the values that matched those being expressed by this young man in his essay, our companies would be demonstrating increased profit while our environment improves. It's called sustainable education folks!

The last essay that Tara shared with us involved a young entrepreneur that simply wanted to run his own business. Because of this assignment he researched some successful startup companies that were working in the field of solar energy. He explained in his essay that the technologies are improving so rapidly that eventually solar energy will be the common source of home heating in the not so distant future. He now has his sights set on studying environmental science in college. Not bad for a one-time English assignment, wouldn't you say?

I thanked Tara for taking the time to share her students' essays with our group. We seemed to have a large number of English teachers in the session so Tara fielded a myriad of content related questions and did so with authority. Tara reminded me of myself many years ago when I thought I was using my knowledge of environmental science as a "crutch" while teaching chemistry because I did not have the typical science teacher's educational experience. As I watched Tara handling those questions, I recalled how much of an advantage that turned out to be.

Vivian teaches her students how to read, write, and speak the language of Chinese, however, she certainly does more than that. Every year she begins the instructional process with an introduction to China's people, their culture, the country itself, and many of the aspects of Chinese society. Until recently, Vivian had steered clear of any negative attributes associated with China, however, after reflecting on that practice, she realized that withholding certain information from her students simply because she felt it might cast a negative impression was not only a missed educational opportunity, it was morally wrong. Vivian stated, "Even if done for the best intentions, failing to provide students with accurate information does them a disservice. How can we expect our students to become well-informed future leaders if we shield them from the truth or impose our own sets of values on them? It is our responsibility to provide our students with the facts and allow them to form their own opinions."

I was thrilled to hear Vivian say those words. One of the most basic concepts addressed in my first book, *Sustainable Education,* is that leaders often base their decisions on their own inherent set of principles. Our educational system has allowed our parents, teachers, and society to imprint values upon us that promote economic growth instead of sustainability. Along with all of the positive aspects of China, Vivian professionally described a truthful account of the environmental problems that face this magnificent country. She explained that these issues are the result of decisions that China's leaders have made based on a value system that promotes economic gain at the expense of environmental health.

Vivian described the massive economic boom that China has experienced in recent decades. Their economic growth coupled with an expanding population resulted in a need for enormous quantities of natural resources. As these resources were extracted, great expanses of earth were degraded, rendering bodies of water and tracks of land useless, and in many cases, toxic and harmful to human health. "Isn't that against the law?" asked one student. "It might be here in the United States," said Vivian, "but China is trying to keep pace with us economically, and regulating these activities would impede those efforts." The students looked amazed. "You mean they would allow people to get sick just to make more money?" asked one young man. I could see that Vivian really wanted to share her personal views on the subject, yet she remained completely factual by responding, "There are many people right here in the United States that want to deregulate and loosen environmental restrictions on industries so that more money can be made."

Vivian told the class, "This is why it is so important for teachers to provide their students with the facts. So many of us grow up with the mentality that the clean air, soil, and water that we enjoy is a right. It's not. It is a privilege and it comes at a cost, an economic one. Our environmental regulations exist to protect our planet as well as our health." "Is that why we see so many pictures of people in China wearing masks?" said one student. Vivian explained that coal is China's main source of energy.

In fact, they are the number one consumer of this non-renewable resource.

Vivian provided a "mini lesson" on the process by which electricity is generated by the burning of fossil fuels. She did an excellent job identifying the primary pollutants that are produced in the process such as oxides of sulfur and nitrogen, mercury, lead, and particulates. She added that carbon dioxide is also produced and that it is considered a greenhouse gas that contributes to climate change. "The masks that you see in those pictures only protect the wearer from particulate matter. They act like a filter," said Vivian. "In those pictures, it looks like the air is actually dirty. Is it really like that?" asked one of the students. Vivian responded, "Unfortunately, that is often the case in major cities like Beijing" (Air Pollution and Health Damages in China, 2007).

Vivian explained that in recent years, environmental groups, formed mostly by young people, are fighting back for their health and that of their children and future generations. She described efforts to pull away from the use of coal and natural gas in the northern areas of the country in order to reduce particulate emissions. She reemphasized that this is not an easy fix. Vivian reminded the students that people have value sets that have been ingrained in them by their societies. If a country's leaders believe that economic growth is more important than providing healthy environmental conditions, positive change can be a very long process.

A student raised his hand and said, "It's great that you are teaching this to us. I have heard people say that we can use 'clean coal' but I learned that's just misleading information so companies can make more money." Vivian responded, "It is good that you are recognizing the value of a sound education. You are becoming eco-literate. In other words, you are able to understand environmental issues and see the impact that human activity can have on the health of our planet." Vivian explained that neither China nor the United States is a sustainable society. She alluded to the fact that the United States has the current economic advantage, which allows for stricter environmental regulations. "This is good for us, but do not take our cleaner environment for granted," she warned. "Hopefully, future leaders will use what is happening in China as an example and avoid making the same mistakes."

Vivian then turned the discussion in a more positive direction. She explained how China is attempting to make sweeping changes in the country's energy policies and in recent years has initiated a massive push toward electric powered vehicles and clean energy sources such as solar power. She spoke of programs in which the government is offering incentives to consumers and manufacturers that partake in these green initiatives. She described the solar and wind energy programs along with the government's heavy investment in infrastructure to support these renewable energy technologies. "In fact," she said, "the success that China is having with some of these efforts in sustainability may actually cause the United States to investigate similar programs" (Chen, G. C., 2017).

As mentioned, Vivian spent several days acquainting her students with the environmental and other aspects of Chinese society. She made her students feel a true connection to the country and its people. It wasn't just another place in the world where people spoke a different language. They really seemed to enjoy the process and were now motivated to learn how to better communicate with their brothers and sisters across the globe. For all they knew, some of them they may one day be working alongside these people.

Vivian revealed both the good and the bad to her students. She provided them with the truth. That is all that anyone can ask of a teacher. We must remember that our students are tomorrow's leaders. I believe that if teachers provide the facts, the next generation will be better prepared to base their decisions on the values they form from that truthful information. As Vivian said, "We should not shield our students from the truth, instead we must arm them with the tools they will need to avoid being misled by unscrupulous individuals who might otherwise attempt to gain from their ignorance." Not only is Vivian an exceptional teacher, she is a positive role model, and a wonderful human being.

Anita teaches English Language Learners (ELL) for her school district. She wished to create a special activity that would not only be a valuable educational experience for her students but one that would also help them feel more comfortable in the transition to their new surroundings. She saw this as a great opportunity to infuse environmental education into her teaching. She asked her students to reflect on the environmental policies and sustainability practices that they experienced in their respective countries before coming to the United States.

She also asked them to observe the environmental policies and sustainability practices demonstrated by the people living here in America. She explained that eventually, she was going to require them to compare the two cultures and identify the differences as well as the similarities in regard to their environmental policies and values.

Before they embarked on this effort, Anita felt that it might be necessary to define and provide a brief introduction to the concepts of sustainability and environmental responsibility. Anita told me that she was surprised to find out how eco-literate her ELL students already were. She described these students as "sustainability-conscious and well ahead of the general population when it comes to environmental awareness." She said that she gained a new appreciation for the need to promote eco-literacy in our American schools after hearing their stories.

Anita invited me to attend one of her classes and explained that most of her ELL students were from Central and South American countries as well the Caribbean Islands. It was very interesting to see the group dynamics as what were originally intended to be individual presentations turned into full class discussions. It appeared as though Anita had struck a chord of similarity for her students and provided a successful educational experience.

The first discussion centered on the availability and use of freshwater. Most of the students were amazed at the differences they observed in water use between their countries and in the United States. "Water seems to be everywhere here and nobody seems to care about how much they use," said one student. Some students said that they did not have hot water back home and they are still getting used to the idea that all they have to do is turn a knob. "If you wanted hot water, you wait for the cistern that collects the rainwater to get warm in the sun," remarked a laughing student. Some of the students were surprised by how long Americans spend in the shower. "We had to take quick showers. You would get in trouble if you wasted water," said a young woman from the Dominican Republic. "When I first saw people putting water on the ground, I thought it was for decoration, like a fountain, but I was told they were watering their lawn," said a student as he shook his head in disbelief.

Soon the discussion turned to the incredible number of cars that exist in the United States. "I couldn't believe that every family has a car," said one student. She was even more surprised to find out that the average American family actually has more than one automobile. "And the cars are all new," said another student as he added, "Have you noticed that they are also really big? In my country the cars are small because gas is expensive and if you have a car you are lucky, so you keep it for as long as you can." One student commented that gasoline can be obtained easily and anytime you want in the United States. "In my country, you only use a car if you have to. People here sometimes use their cars just for fun," said a student from Honduras.

Anita's school is located right outside of New York City and some of the students commented that since they were already used to relying on public transportation, they had no problem getting around using buses. They noted that their peers were not so adept at using mass transit since most of them had their own cars. "I still can't believe that my neighbor comes home with a car full of groceries at least twice a week," said a student.

That comment helped the dialogue morph into the readily available and affordable food. "The family that I stayed with when I first came here laughed when they took me to a 7-11 store and I commented how lucky they were to have such an unbelievable place that had almost everything so they took me to see another place called Costco. I could not believe that so many things were available in one place," said a girl from Guatemala.

The discussion then focused on where all of these materials go after people use them. The class discussed the colorful packages that supplies come in. "Why do people here go through all of the trouble to put things in these packages just to throw the coverings away as soon as they get home? Why not just buy something and put it in your own bag? That's what we do. This way seems to make no sense," said one student. Most of the students were taught at an early age that nothing was to be wasted. A boy explained how, whenever they were lucky enough to find a plastic water bottle, they either used it over and over or found some other useful purpose for the item. Other students remarked that it was amazing that a truck comes and takes away very usable items several times each week. "We always used food wastes as either fertilizer or for animal feed. The only items that we actually threw away were things for which we could find absolutely no other use," said one student. Another student commented, "In my country you had to pay someone to take away your garbage. Most people just let the stuff pile up. Almost everyone had their own pile that stayed around for years." "I still feel bad when I go to the cafeteria here," said a student from Haiti. She continued, "I know this sounds terrible but when I see my classmates throw away so much good food, I think about how that could have fed people back in my country."

"I never had red meat before coming here," said one student who was immediately agreed with by several others. Anita explained that pound per pound, beef requires much more energy to produce than poultry. She asked them to think about how much food one cow needs to eat and how much it has to drink in its lifetime. She also pointed out that producing the feed for the cows requires huge amounts of water. As a result, red meat is a poor choice for human beings when it comes to efficiently meeting our nutritional requirements. Anita said, "Red meat can be considered a food for the wealthy. In your biology classes you will learn that 90% of an organism's energy is lost every time you move up a trophic level in a food chain." Almost every student looked puzzled by her last statement. "Forget it," she said laughing, "let's just say that eating red meat wastes a lot of water and energy. There are much better ways of getting the protein we need."

A boy from Nicaragua said, "I noticed that even teachers in this school don't turn out the lights when they leave a room. In my country, blackouts and brownouts are common and you can't even rely on energy to be available. In my school we had solar energy that only lasted for a certain amount of time so the lights were turned off whenever possible to conserve." Almost all of the students agreed that their American peers do not even seem to notice that energy is being wasted.

The last student to speak had been quiet all period. She stood up and said, "I can't believe how clean everything is here. Your streams are clear and your air smells good. I lived by a factory that had a pipe that put red liquid into the stream near my home. This was our water supply and people were getting sick but there was nothing that we could do about it. That is why my parents wanted to come here. I would do anything to stay here and keep this place as beautiful as it is."

I only wish that every teacher and every American for that matter could have been there to hear what that young lady had said. Her simple, spontaneous, and heartfelt appreciation for what we have and often take for granted was refreshing to witness. Already aware that such a dream may not be possible, she expressed her desire to help keep this way of living a reality. The problem is that this young woman already understands what so many of us do not. Common sense tells us that our society and way of life is not sustainable. Perhaps, with the help of her future teachers that will choose to take environmental education as seriously as her ELL instructor does, this student may someday get her wish.

Britney handles the upper level English courses for her high school. In her unit that deals with primary research, Britney decided to make sustainability the overarching theme for her students' critical essays. She instructed her students to research any topic that related to sustainability, develop a thesis statement, and support that statement using information they obtain from valid sources. This was the first time that Britney had used sustainability as her research theme. Based on how motivated, accurate, and well written the resulting essays were, she reported that she was going to establish this as an educational goal the next time the curriculum is revised. The following are summaries of a few of the essays that Britney shared with us.

One student's thesis stated, "A larger problem than the environmental crisis itself, is the reality that our society does not agree that an environmental crisis exists." Among others, the student detailed environmental issues such as climate change, overpopulation, resource depletion, and environmental degradation. He cited numerous, credible sources documenting these issues as major problems facing our society and threatening sustainability and our way of life. However, he cleverly balanced each statement with an actual counter argument made by powerful individuals that maintain a planetary management ideology. The student argued that these people have, and continue to use their influence to promote the idea that human beings have the right to alter the planet as they see fit. He explained that these individuals feel that human beings have the intelligence and ability to mitigate any potential crisis, environmental or otherwise, that may appear. The student's essay cleverly described a future society that continued to debate the role that human beings should play on the planet right up until a point where human beings no longer exist due to their inability to recognize the gravity of the situation that they are in. In his essay, the student referred to the often-told story of the frog in boiling water. The idea is that if you put a frog in a pot of boiling water it will jump out, but if you put the same frog in temperate water and slowly raise the temperature, the frog will boil to death because it never realized the point at which it was in danger. The boy did an outstanding job comparing our society to the frog. He concluded that unless we can agree that we are experiencing an environmental crisis and must learn to live sustainably, we have a lot more to worry about than just the environmental problems we face, as obviously real as they may be.

A second essay's thesis was delivered in the form of a question, "Do we have a moral and ethical responsibility to control the exponential growth of human population?" The interesting point the student brought up was the ignorance that so many people have to this topic, even though it is the root cause of many of our environmental problems. She defined the issues and presented compelling data that definitively supported the existence of a crisis. Her essay clearly identified the undeniable, eventual collapse of the human species should our population continue to expand at its current rate. Although she identified potential catastrophes capable of returning our population to its natural carrying capacity such as war, pandemics, food shortages, deterioration of living conditions, and the scarcity of water, the student carefully avoided predicting which of these scenarios will be the one to occur. She expertly introduced solutions that at first seem morally and ethically questionable, especially when one considers the beliefs held sacred by some of the world's most prevalent religions. The student critically addressed a problem that is intentionally but not admittedly ignored by our society, because the truth is, there is no simple solution. She ended her essay with, "If we continue to ignore the laws of nature, eventually nature will make adjustments, and we may not be part of the solution."

Another student stated, "A lack of common sense has led to the economic collapse of entire countries." In this essay, the student defined natural and economic capital. He explained that although not equivalent from an economic standpoint, every human society begins with natural resources that are associated with their environment. He compared this to a "hand" that one may be dealt in a poker game and how the individual plays their hand is crucial. He provided an example of two countries that share a common border, and for all intents and purposes, once enjoyed similar natural capital. However, one of the countries exploited its natural resources in a manner that would maximize the immediate economic return while the other placed restrictions on those resources. Today, one of the countries is considered a premiere travel destination and the other viewed as one of the poorest nations in the world. Applying probability, the student provided a statistical argument that the drastic divergence of these societies was clearly the result of one country's inability to see beyond the immediate and employ the common-sense environmental restrictions imposed by its neighbor.

A very interesting essay examined how our society isolates itself from the rest of the world. The student's thesis stated, "Human beings have created a false sense of separation from nature by being the only species that fails to follow two rules of sustainability." This student explained the first principle of sustainability maintains that energy from the sun is used directly by every living organism on our planet. He maintained that we violate this principle as we have found ways to use solar energy that has been stored in the ground in the form of fossil fuels. The student argued that if human beings never exploited fossil fuels, our species would already be living in a sustainable manner and many of the current environmental issues that face our society would either be negligible or non-existent. The student supported his argument with reputable data pertaining to the contribution of fossil fuel use to issues such as overpopulation, air, water, and soil pollution, environmental degradation, climate change, and resource depletion. The student proposed, "Imagine if the Native American culture was able to continue without interference and fossil fuels were never discovered. What would America look like today?" That statement really made me appreciate his point. The student also explained the fact that every species other than our own takes only what it needs in order to survive. We on the other hand, place value on possessions. This unnatural greed has resulted in a breakdown in the natural recycling process of minerals and chemical substances, a second fundamental principle of sustainability. The student provided several documented examples for which natural systems were disrupted by the removal of essential nutrients. He stated,

"Obvious common sense is lost in our ignorance and feeling of self-importance."

One final essay asked the simple question, "Will human nature permit a sustainable future for our species?" This student proposed what appeared to be a purely philosophical question, however, she provided an answer based solely on scientific fact. Step by step, and beginning with what are considered to be human ancestors, the student methodically introduced the societal responses to changing environmental conditions. She carefully documented a number of the major and significant "advances" in human society. Each supported her theory that, when confronted with the choice, our species opts for selfishness as opposed to altruism. She argued that science has proven that a species needs only to act out of self-preservation. However, the degradation of our planet caused by uncounted generations of human greed and selfish activity can only be regenerated by an equal number of generations exhibiting true altruistic behavior. Since there are no significant examples of global altruistic human behavior in recorded human history, this student concluded that the statistical probability of our species demonstrating the self-sacrificing actions necessary for ensuring a sustainable future is depressingly low.

Although I disagree with the last student's conclusion and hold a much more optimistic vision for our future, I certainly can appreciate her opinion as she very accurately delineated the problem and supported all of her views with scientific evidence. The good news is that the final story of our species has not yet been written. In fact, Britney and language teachers around the globe that choose to promote eco-literacy in their classrooms will provide a forum for the next generation to read, analyze, discuss, and write their own future. The future indeed belongs to them and so does the truth about our failures. When I asked Britney what she thought about this assignment she said, "I cried when I read some of these essays. These kids poured their hearts and souls into researching these topics and expressing and supporting their ideas. It gave me hope, but it also gave me inspiration. This is why I became a teacher in the first place." Britney is certainly using language as a scientific tool.

Chapter 12 – This is Everyone's Business

I hope that you have enjoyed reading this small sampling of how incredible teachers across the United States are infusing environmental education into their instruction. As you can see, it's happening in every grade level and every discipline in America's schools as well as educational programs throughout the world. If your school is already engaged in producing eco-literate graduates that is wonderful. If not, perhaps it is time to ask your school leaders to read *Sustainable Education,* or hand them this copy of *Sea, It's Happening.*

It may be unfair to immediately condemn the intentions of decision makers for failing to promote eco-literacy, especially if they are older folks like me. Please remember that the values we cling to have been ingrained in us by our teachers, families, and society at a very young age. Today's leaders often make decisions based on those principles that many times, do not hold sustainability to be as important a consideration as economic growth. I guess it all comes down to one simple question, "What is success?" Hopefully, the stories that you have read in this book have caused you to reflect on that question. One thing that I can tell you for sure is that success is certainly not the demise of our society. It is not the extinction of thousands of species from our planet. It is not departing from this world the wealthiest individual that has failed to contribute to the health and welfare of others.

I've observed many teachers contribute to the betterment of this world. These efforts have come in many different forms and sometimes from directions that I never would have imagined. The final story that I would like to share is a special one because it promises hope for our children. It speaks a truth that if heard by enough, can truly tip the scales in favor of a sustainable future. Nearly every corporate leader in charge of making critical policy decisions that has heard it has agreed with its indisputably accurate and undeniable message.

Doug is the quintessential, veteran teacher beloved by his students, colleagues, administration and community. You will see him at nearly every extracurricular event and he can't seem to say no whenever a student asks for help. He loves teaching business and finance and it shows. Doug was once an extremely successful corporate leader and financial expert. Many people wonder why he is teaching at a public high school. I asked him point blank and he told me, "I left the private sector so that I could give something back after years of just taking." That is all he said as he handed me a stack of final exams. "Read the students' answers to the take home essay," he said. I started reading and looked up at him. He was already smiling at me. I finished the first, and began reading another. I flipped through a few more and said, "You're doing it." "I know," he responded with a twinkle in his eye.

What people don't know about Doug is that prior to his successful run in business, he had studied as an environmental scientist. He has always been passionate about environmental issues, understands them, and was born to help others. Only a "lucky, once in a lifetime opportunity" offered to him many years ago steered him down a different life journey. He eventually had to cut ties with that path in order to attain true happiness and rediscover the legacy that he wanted to leave. Doug pointed to the papers and said with genuine pride, "See that? Now that is what true success looks like," as he patted his chest.

Heck, I would have certainly failed this final exam. It asked about things like stock market productivity and profit, forms of business organizations, inflation and deflation, fiscal policies, world economic strategies, trade deficits, exchange rates, and regulations pertaining to labor unions to name only a few. That take-home essay question, however, I would have aced and so did his students. The problem is that the majority of today's decision makers may not have gotten it correct. Therein lies the true difference that Doug is making. He is creating eco-literate business leaders. The question read, "Based on what you have learned in class, explain what you believe to be the largest flaw in our society's economic system, the potential impacts of that imperfection, and a possible solution. Be sure to fully support your statement."

The responses that Doug received from his last set of classes were truly inspirational. Allow me to reproduce one student's response that was, what I believe to be, exceptional. I have corrected some spelling and grammar, however, this was the gist of his answer:

The largest flaw in our society's economic system is our failure to include the loss of natural capital in our financial calculations. The potential impacts of this imperfection are environmental degradation, ecosystem destruction, and the inevitable collapse of our society. A possible solution would be to pass the cost of restoring our Earth's natural capital on to the consumer.

When I was ten years old my parents took me on a vacation cruise. Although I shouldn't have been allowed to do so, nobody stopped me from sneaking into the casino and playing the slots. I asked my dad for some money and he gave me $20 in quarters. Every time the machine paid out, I put the winnings in my pocket. When I had played the last of the original quarters, I went back and told my dad that I was out of money, and of course, I said nothing about the coins that were in my pocket. He gave me another $20 that I immediately played until gone, and again placed all of the coins that came out of the machine in my pocket. I told my dad that I used all of his quarters and asked for more. This time he said, "No" and asked me if I learned a good lesson about gambling. Later that night I returned to our cabin and showed my mom the $26 that I had "Won" in the casino. She told me that I was pretty lucky and said, "Your father will be impressed." I told her not to tell him!

Natural capital is the world's stock of assets from which humans derive a wide range of what our current economic system considers "free" goods and services. Examples of these free goods are fossil fuels, lumber, and minerals. Examples of free services include erosion control, pollination, and purification of our air, water, and soil. However, I will demonstrate that these goods and services should not be considered free, just as the quarters that my father supplied me with on the cruise should not have been regarded as free as they were certainly an integral factor in my gambling experience.

Our society functions on growth-based economic calculations, however, the factors that we use in our calculations represent only a portion of the entire system. In general, we extract resources from the Earth, process these raw materials, market the products, sell them, and recycle or discard any waste that is produced. We define increases in our economic capital as our profit and credit ourselves with having grown as a society. However, as our economic capital increases our natural capital decreases. In the short term, as we are currently experiencing at this point in the evolution of our species, this does not even seem to be an issue because the Earth's resources are indeed enormous. My family certainly did not end up homeless because I swindled my dad out of $40 on that cruise. However, what if, for the rest of my life, I continued to take money from my father, whose income sustained my family, and I failed to pay him back? Common sense tells us that eventually, my entire family would be in serious trouble.

This is no different from our treatment of the Earth and it's natural capital. As we have learned in class this year, we rely on the Earth's resources and services for our very existence. Continuing to function using our current growth-based economic system will ultimately result in natural capital becoming so depleted that the entire process will cease to function.

In conclusion, our growth-based economic system is illogical since it is unsustainable. It relies on goods and services being supplied by the Earth and fails to account for their costs. Only an adjustment in our economic calculations that establishes a means by which the environmental degradation caused by human activities is restored will result in a more sustainable process. In order to solve this problem, the costs for these restoration efforts must be passed on to the consumer establishing a viable system that can continue in perpetuity. It will mean a societal sacrifice, but that is necessary if our way of life is to continue.

I'm certainly not an economic guru but I loved that student's essay response and the perfect analogy it provided for how our society treats the very Earth that supports us. While the child in the casino considered himself a winner, it is obvious that everyone, especially his father, had lost.

"These kids wrote these essays on their own?" I asked Doug in disbelief. "They did," he said "but getting them prepared to do so by making them eco-literate was the key." "What's your secret?" I asked him. Doug responded, "It's no secret. I read your book *Sustainable Education* and I agree with everything in it. I've been infusing environmental education into my teaching for years. Whenever possible, I work some interesting idea or concept into my lessons. It's amazing how relevant the field of sustainability is to business and economics and it also makes everything more interesting for the kids."

Doug made me aware of the World Economic Forum that met in 2019 in Davos, Switzerland. At that conference, for the first time, an organization known as the

Natural Capital Finance Alliance (NCFA) prepared a step-by-step guide for financial institutions to assist them in understanding the complexity of natural capital. Five different world banks piloted the guide, which recognizes the economic disruption that is occurring as the depletion of natural resources accelerates. The guide identifies ways in which businesses depend on the environment (What Do Companies Owe The Environment? Natural Capital Risk Assessment At Davos, 2019).

In parting Doug said, "See, it's happening whether anyone likes it or not, and I'm doing what I can to get these kids ready for their future. I will certainly continue to teach all of the basics that are so carefully detailed in the business and finance curriculum; however, I will make sure that my students know how to use and apply that knowledge in a society that must redefine how it measures success."

Doug is doing his part to develop future leaders that are not only capable of succeeding in a competitive world but will serve as positive role models promoting a sustainability-conscious society. To me, Doug's story remains a special one, for it is my experience that the individuals who most resist the sacrifices necessary for a transition to a sustainable society are those that have the most to lose from an economic standpoint. However, it is our planet, our society, and our children that concern me, not the "bottom lines" of the companies owned by the elite few that demand that "The American Way of Life" is non-negotiable.

Sea, It's Happening has only scratched the surface of what so many incredible teachers have done in regard to sustainability education. As I reflect on the plethora of lessons, programs, and activities that I have witnessed and the thousands of dedicated teachers that are paving the way for a sustainable future for our children, I stand in awe. Whether you teach elementary, middle, or high school; regardless if your discipline is social studies, mathematics, science, English, foreign language, the arts, physical education, or business; you are teachers. I know why most of you entered this profession in the first place. Just like me, you want to make a difference. Well, here is your chance to make the biggest difference that our society will ever need to achieve, and it's the one that needs to occur in order for our way of life to continue.

Please ask yourself, "What is success?" For me, it means every citizen becoming eco-literate. It means every teacher striving to infuse environmental education into his or her instruction. It means every child being provided with the truth about the environmental crises that threaten their world and being provided the tools needed to combat these issues. It means that every person realizes that sustainability is everyone's business.

Sea, It's Happening!

If you would like to have additional information in regard to any lesson or idea presented in this book, or if there is any way that Sustainable Education Associates can assist you, your school, or your district in producing eco-literate graduates, please do not hesitate to e-mail me, Dr. Joseph Soporowski directly at seayourfuture@gmail.com or call me at 732-575-7359.

References and Resources

About the Sustainable Development Goals - United Nations
        Sustainable Development. (2015). Retrieved from
        https://www.un.org/sustainabledevelopment/sustainable-
        development-goals/
Air Pollution and Health Damages in China. (2007). Clearing the
        Air. doi:10.7551/mitpress/1866.003.0005
Albajes, R. (2013). Integrated Pest Management. Sustainable Food
        Production, 1003-1034. doi:10.1007/978-1-4614-5797-
        8_164
Alternative Farming Systems Information Center. (n.d.). Retrieved
        from https://www.nal.usda.gov/afsic
Andersen, I. (2015, January 28). Failing to protect nature's capital
        could cost businesses trillions. Retrieved March 12, 2017,
        from https://www.theguardian.com/sustainable-
        business/2015/jan/28/natural-captial-profit-world-economy
Applegate, J. S., & Laitos, J. (2006). Environmental law: RCRA,
        CERCLA, and the management of hazardous waste. New
        York, NY: Foundation Press.
Aronoff, K., (2019, March 05). How Greta Thunberg's Lone Strike
        Against Climate Change Became a Global Movement.
        Retrieved from
        https://www.rollingstone.com/politics/politics-
        features/greta-thunberg-fridays-for-future-climate-change-
        800675/
Biotechnology FAQs. (n.d.). Retrieved from
        https://www.usda.gov/topics/biotechnology /biotechnology-
        frequently-asked-questions-faqs
CDC - Respirators - NIOSH Workplace Safety and Health Topic.
        (n.d.). Retrieved 2019, from
        https://www.cdc.gov/niosh/topics/respirators/default.html

294

Chen, G. C. (2017). Renewable Energy Development in East China. Current Sustainable/Renewable Energy Reports, 4(2), 33-37. doi:10.1007/s40518-017-0067-3

Creamer, A. E., & Gao, B. (2015). Overview of Greenhouse Gases and Global Warming. SpringerBriefs in Molecular Science Carbon Dioxide Capture: An Effective Way to Combat Global Warming, 1-15.

Crewe, K., & Forsyth, A. (2011). Compactness and Connection in Environmental Design: Insights from Ecoburbs and Ecocities for Design with Nature. Environment and Planning B: Planning and Design, 38(2), 267-288.

Daily, G. C., & Ehrlich, P. R. (1994). Population, Sustainability, and Earth's Carrying Capacity. Ecosystem Management, 435-450. doi:10.1007/978-1-4612-4018-1_32

Douglass, A., Newman, P. A., & Solomon, S. (2014, July). The Antarctic ozone hole: An update: Physics Today: Vol 67, No 7. Retrieved from http://physicstoday.scitation.org/doi/10.1063/PT.3.2449

Dresner, S. (2012). The Principles of Sustainability. doi:10.4324/9781849773249

Ehrlich, P. R., & Holdren, J. P. (1971). Impact of Population Growth. Science, 171(3977), 1212-1217. doi:10.1126/science.171.3977.1212

Emergency Planning and Community Right-to-Know Act (EPCRA). (2014). Encyclopedia of Toxicology, 320. doi:10.1016/b978-0-12-386454-3.01228-8

Ergonomics for Schools. (n.d.). Retrieved from http://www.ergonomics4schools.com/lzone/seating.htm

Espenshade, T. J., Ehrlich, P. R., & Ehrlich, A. H. (1991). The Population Explosion. Population and Development Review, 17(2), 331. doi:10.2307/1973735

Everything You Need To Know About The Tesla Powerwall 2 (2019 Edition). (2019, January 22). Retrieved from https://cleantechnica.com/2019/01/19/everything-you-need-to-know-about-the-powerwall-2-2019-edition/

Fattouh, T. N. (2017). Climate Change And The Mayan Collapse: High Resolution Paleoclimate Reconstruction From Speleothem Records In Belize. doi:10.1130/abs/2017sc-289614

Fawell, J. (2010). *Drinking water safety and standards for drinking water. Environmental Medicine, 290-296. doi:10.1201/b13390-32*

Finlayson, C. M. (2016). *Climate Change: United Nations Framework Convention on Climate Change (UNFCCC) and Intergovernmental Panel for Climate Change (IPCC). The Wetland Book, 1-5. doi:10.1007/978-94-007-6172-8_127-1*

Foster, W. M., & Costa, D. L. (2005). *Air pollutants and the respiratory tract. Boca Raton: Taylor & Francis.*

Fulford, R. S., Russell, M., Harvey, J., & Harwell, M. C. (2016). *Sustainability at the Community Level: Searching for Common Ground as Part of a National Strategy for Decision Support (R-16 ed., Vol. 600, Ser. 178, p. 153) (USA, Environmental Protection Agency, National Service Center for Environmental Publications).*

Gessen, M. (2018, October 2). *The Fifteen Year-Old Climate Activist Who is Demanding a New Kind of Politics. The New Yorker. Retrieved February 15, 2019, from https://www.newyorker.com/news/our-columnists/the-fifteen-year-old-climate-activist-who-is-demanding-a-new-kind-of-politics*

Goldsmith, J. (1968). *Effects of Air Pollution on Human Health. Air Pollution and Its Effects, 547-615. doi:10.1016/b978-0-12-666551-2.50021-2*

Goodland, R. J., Daly, H. E., & Serafy, S. E. (1992). *Population, technology, and lifestyle: The transition to sustainability. Washington, D.C.: Island Press.*

Goyal, P., & Gurtoo, S. (2011). *Factors Influencing Public Perception: Genetically Modified Organisms. GMO Biosafety Research. doi:10.5376/gmo.2011.02.0001*

Green careers: Choosing work for a sustainable future. (2010). *Choice Reviews Online, 47(05). doi:10.5860/choice.*

Groot, R. D., Brander, L., Ploeg, S. V., Costanza, R., Bernard, F., Braat, L., . . . Beukering, P. V. (2012). *Global estimates of the value of ecosystems and their services in monetary units. Ecosystem Services, 1(1), 50-61. doi:10.1016/j.ecoser.2012.07.005*

Guidelines On Design of Noise Barriers. (n.d.). Retrieved from
   https://www.epd.gov.hk/epd/english/environmentinhk/noise/
   guide_ref/design_barriers_content2.html.

Hanks, T. W., & Swiegers, G. F. (2012). Introduction: The Concept
   of Biomimicry and Bioinspiration in Chemistry.
   Bioinspiration and Biomimicry in Chemistry, 1-15.
   doi:10.1002/9781118310083.ch1

Hardin, G. (2009). The Tragedy of the Commons. Journal of Natural
   Resources Policy Research, 1(3), 243-253.
   doi:10.1080/19390450903037302

Hartmann, T. (2004). The last hours of ancient sunlight: The fate of
   the world and what we can do before it's too late. New
   York: Three Rivers Press.

Hirvilammi, T., & Helne, T. (2014). Changing Paradigms: A Sketch
   for Sustainable Wellbeing and Ecosocial Policy.
   Sustainability, 6(4), 2160-2175. doi:10.3390/su6042160

Holzman, D. C. (2012). Accounting for Nature's Benefits: The
   Dollar Value of Ecosystem Services. Environmental Health
   Perspectives, 120(4).

Images, D. W. (2017, October 19). Acid Rain. Retrieved from
   https://www.nationalgeographic.com/environment/global-
   warming/acid-rain/

Jaffe, J. L., & Stavins, R. N. (2008). Linking a U.S. Cap-and-Trade
   System for Greenhouse Gas Emissions: Opportunities,
   Implications, and Challenges. SSRN Electronic Journal.
   doi:10.2139/ssrn.1089042

Jarman, C., Guzmán, A. J., Fernández-Pérez, N. A., Svoboda, E., &
   Follis, K. (2018, March 27). What Really Happened on
   Easter Island? Retrieved from
   https://www.sapiens.org/archaeology/easter-island-demise/

Kart, J. (2018, July 30). Bracelets Fund Ocean Cleanup, 1 Million
   Pounds And Counting. Retrieved from
   https://www.forbes.com/sites/jeffkart/2018/07/30/bracelets-
   fund-ocean-cleanup-1-million-pounds-and-counting/

Kolb, V. (1993). Registry Of Toxic Effects Of Chemical Substances
   As A Source For Compiling A List Of Teratogens.
   Teratogens, 116-581. doi:10.1016/b978-0-444-81482-
   1.50010-4

Kolbert, E. (2015). Sixth extinction: An unnatural history. London:
   Bloomsbury.

Koning, N. (2017). *Food Security, Agricultural Policies and Economic Growth. doi:10.4324/9781315753928*

Kotz, J. C., & Treichel, P. M. (2018, October 16). *Chemical reaction. Retrieved from https://www.britannica.com/science/chemical-reaction*

Kunicki, R. (1987). *OSHA Noise Exposure Measurements. SAE Technical Paper Series. doi:10.4271/870957*

Lang, W. W. (1981). *Standards for Noise Measurements. Noise Control Engineering, 16(1), 37. doi:10.3397/1.2832170*

Larson, A., & York, J. (2017). *Nike: Moving Down the Sustainability Track Through Chemical Substitution and Waste Reduction. Darden Business Publishing Cases, 1(1), 1-4. doi:10.1108/case.darden.2016.000215*

Leakey, R. E., & Lewin, R. (1996). *The sixth extinction: Patterns of life and the future of humankind. New York: Anchor Books.*

Learn About Sustainability. (2016, October 18). *Retrieved from https://www.epa.gov/sustainability/learn-about-sustainability*

Lee, K. (2019, January 10). *The Disadvantages of Nuclear Energy. Retrieved from https://sciencing.com/disadvantages-nuclear-energy-4578885.html*

Liu, S. X. (2014). *Biological wastewater treatment processes. Food and Agricultural Wastewater Utilization and Treatment, 103-132. doi:10.1002/9781118353967.ch4*

Logan, E. (2015, June 2). *10 reasons clean coal is a marketing myth. Retrieved from http://www.environmentalhealthnews.org/ehs/news/2015/jun/10-reasons-clean-coal-is-a-marketing-myth*

Magill, B. (2016, August 03). *Artificial Leaf Turns CO2 Emissions Into Fuel. Retrieved from https://www.climatecentral.org/news/artificial-leaf-turns-co2-into-fuel-20577*

Magill, B. (2016, November 18). *Scientists Take Big Step Toward Safely Burying CO2. Retrieved from http://www.climatecentral.org/news/scientists-take-big-step-toward-safely-burying-co2-20896*

Magill, B. (2017, May 31). *World's First Commercial CO2 Capture Plant Goes Live. Retrieved from https://www.climatecentral.org/news/first-commercial-co2-capture-plant-live-21494*

298

Malakoff, D. (2015). By 98 to 1, U.S. Senate passes amendment
    saying climate change is real, not a hoax. Science.
    doi:10.1126/science.aaa6378

Managing Air Quality - Ambient Air Monitoring. (2018, August 28).
    Retrieved from https://www.epa.gov/air-quality-
    management-process/managing-air-quality-ambient-air-
    monitoring

Miller, G. T., & Spoolman, S. (2015). Living in the environment:
    Principles, connections, and solutions. Stamford, CT:
    Cengage Learning.

Mcnicoll, G. (2015). IPAT (Impact, Population, Affluence, and
    Technology). International Encyclopedia of the Social &
    Behavioral Sciences, 716-718. doi:10.1016/b978-0-08-
    097086-8.91045-6

Mogelgaard, K. (2015, December 23). What Does the Paris
    Agreement Mean for Climate Resilience and Adaptation?
    Retrieved from https://www.newsecuritybeat.org/
    2016/01/paris-agreement-climate-resilience-adaptation/

Mohaddes, K. (2013). Econometric modeling of world oil supplies:
    Terminal price and the time to depletion. OPEC Energy
    Review, 37(2), 162-193. doi:10.1111/opec.12012

Moses, C. O. (1989). A Geochemical Perspective on the Causes and
    Periodicity of Mass Extinctions. Ecology, 70(4), 812-823.
    doi:10.2307/1941350

Nevers, N. D. (2017). Air pollution control engineering. Long Grove,
    IL: Waveland Press.

Noblet, C., Lindenfeld, L., & Anderson, M. (2013). Environmental
    Worldviews: A Point of Common Contact, or Barrier?
    Sustainability, 5(11), 4825-4842. doi:10.3390/su5114825

Nordic Council of Ministers. (2013). Five approaches to account for
    natural capital and biodiversity. Natural Capital in a
    Nordic Context TemaNord, 29-59.
    doi:10.6027/9789289329491-5-en

Overview of Greenhouse Gases. (2018, October 31). Retrieved from
    https://www.epa.gov/ghgemissions/overview-greenhouse-
    gases

Prugh, T., Costanza, R., Cumberland, J., Daly, H. E., Goodland, R.,
    & Norgaard, R. E. (1999). What Natural Capital Is and
    Does. Ecological Economics Natural Capital and Human

Economic Survival, Second Edition.
doi:10.1201/9781420048322.sec2

Rapp, D. (2014). Anthropogenic Influences on Climate Change.
Assessing Climate Change, 533-595.

Rehm, S., Gros, E., & Jansen, G. (1985). Effects of noise on health
and well-being. Stress Medicine, 1(3), 183-191.
doi:10.1002/smi.2460010308

Resource Conservation and Recovery Act (RCRA) Laws and
Regulations. (2017, January 04). Retrieved from
https://www.epa.gov/rcra

Richman, B. (2015). Historic Climate Agreement Reached in Paris.
Eos, 96. doi:10.1029/2015eo041471

Schoemaker, J. M., & Vitale, C. Y. (1991). Healthy homes, healthy
kids: Protecting your children from everyday environmental
hazards. Washington, D.C.: Island Press.

Schroedl, C. J., Go, L. H., & Cohen, R. A. (2016). Coal Mine Dust
Lung Disease: The Silent Coal Mining Disaster. Current
Respiratory Medicine Reviews, 12(1), 65-73.
doi:10.2174/1573398x11666151026222347

Shapiro, J. (2015, September 24). How Shakespeare's great escape
from the plague changed theatre. Retrieved from
https://www.theguardian.com/books/2015/sep/24/shakespea
res-great-escape-plague-1606--james-shapiro

Sharifi, A. (2016). From Garden City to Eco-urbanism: The quest
for sustainable neighborhood development. Sustainable
Cities and Society, 20, 1-16. doi:10.1016/j.scs.2015.09.002

Sholarin, E. A., & Awange, J. L. (2015). Environmental Risk and
Decision Analysis. Environmental Science and Engineering
Environmental Project Management, 137-161.
doi:10.1007/978-3-319-27651-9_7

Short, R. (1999). Did agriculture cause the population explosion?
Nature, 397(6715), 101-101. doi:10.1038/16339-c1

Sohn, E. (2014, June 24). A Spider's Silky Strength. Retrieved from
https://www.sciencenewsforstudents.org/article/spiders-
silky-strength

Soporowski, J. J. (2017). Sustainable education: A simplistic
strategy for infusing environmental education into
Americas schools. United States: SEA. LLC.

Sorenson, B. (2012). Hydrogen and fuel cells: Emerging
technologies and applications. Oxford: Academic Press.

Stephenson, M. (2015). *Shale gas and fracking: The science behind the controversy. Amsterdam (Holanda): Elsevier.*

Streeten, P. P. (1988). *World economic growth: Case studies of developed and developing nations. Journal of Comparative Economics, 12(3), 450-453. doi:10.1016/0147-5967(88)90091-1*

Teixeira, S., & Zuberi, A. (2016). *Mapping the Racial Inequality in Place: Using Youth Perceptions to Identify Unequal Exposure to Neighborhood Environmental Hazards. International Journal of Environmental Research and Public Health, 13(9), 844. doi:10.3390/ijerph13090844*

The Intergovernmental Panel on Climate Change. (n.d.). *Retrieved from https://www.ipcc.ch/*

Tsakas, M. P., Siskos, A. P., & Siskos, P. A. (2011). *Indoor Air Pollutants and the Impact on Human Health. Chemistry, Emission Control, Radioactive Pollution and Indoor Air Quality. doi:10.5772/18806*

United Nations. (2017, August 18). *Sustainable Development Goals: Improve Life All Around The Globe. Retrieved from https://www.youtube.com/watch?v=kGcrYkHwE80*

U.S. Department of Labor. (n.d.). *Retrieved from https://www.osha.gov/Publications/OSHA3514.html*

U.S. and World Population Clock. (n.d.). *Retrieved from https://www.census.gov/popclock/*

U.S. Department of Commerce, & NOAA National Centers for Environmental Information. (2018, October 03). *National Centers for Environmental Information. Retrieved from http://www.nodc.noaa.gov/*

U.S. Green Building Council: LEED. (n.d.). *Retrieved from http://www.usgbc.org/*

Veghte, B. W. (2015). *Social Inequality, Retirement Security, and the Future of Social Security. Poverty & Public Policy, 7(2), 97-122. doi:10.1002/pop4.104*

Vellend, M. (2017). *Are local losses of biodiversity causing degraded ecosystem function? Oxford Scholarship Online. doi:10.1093/oso/9780198808978.003.0004*

Vercillo, K. (2012, October 30). *Eco Cities: What They Are And Where In the World to Find Them. Retrieved from http://hubpages.com/travel/Ecocities-What-They-Are-And-Where-To-Find-Them*

Viessman, W. (2009). Water supply and pollution control. Upper Saddle River (New Jersey): Pearson Education.

Wallace, M. (2008). The way we will be 50 years from today: 60 of the world's greatest minds share their visions of the next half century. Nashville, TN: Thomas Nelson.

Ways of Expressing Concentration. (2018, November 26). Retrieved from https://chem.libretexts.org /Bookshelves/General_Chemistry/Map:_Chemistry_- _The_Central_Science_(Brown_et_al.)/13:_Properties_of_ Solutions/13.4:_Ways_of_Expressing_Concentration

What a Waste: An Updated Look into the Future of Solid Waste Management. (2018, September). Retrieved from https://www.worldbank.org/en/news/immersive- story/2018/09/20/what-a-waste-an-updated-look-into-the- future-of-solid-waste-management

What Do Companies Owe The Environment? Natural Capital Risk Assessment At Davos. (2019, January 16). Retrieved from https://cleantechnica.com/2019/01/16/what-do-companies- owe-the-environment-natural-capital-risk-assessment-at- davos/

What is Renewable Energy? Sources of Renewable Energy. (2019) Retrieved from http://www.eschooltoday.com/energy/renewable- energy/what-is-renewable-energy.html

What is Sustainable Forestry? (2016, July 28). Retrieved from https://www.rainforest-alliance.org/articles/what-is- sustainable-forestry

Willemsen, M. C. (2018). Tobacco Industry Influence. Tobacco Control Policy in the Netherlands, 183-230. doi:10.1007/978-3-319-72368-6_8

Wright, S. A. (1993). The nimby syndrome: Exploring the relationship between public education and siting opposition. Waste Management, 13(5-7), 538. doi:10.1016/0956-053x(93)90136-k

Zaillian, S., Rudin, S., Redford, R., Pfeffer, R., Travolta, J., Duvall, R., Fry, S., ... Buena Vista Home Entertainment (Firm),. (1999). A Civil Act

Index

ABOUT THE AUTHOR

Dr. Joseph J. Soporowski is the Director of Academic and Environmental Programs with Sustainable Education Associates, LLC, a New Jersey based environmental and educational consulting firm. He is an Ambassador for the United Nations, TeachSDGs (Sustainable Development Goals) Program and a leading advocate for sustainability education. He is the author of the educational primer, *Sustainable Education – A Simplistic Strategy For Infusing Environmental Education Into America's Schools.* Dr. Soporowski received his doctorate in Environmental Sciences in 1991 from Rutgers University. After serving as a faculty member for the Rutgers Department of Environmental Sciences, he acquired field experience as an environmental consultant in his professional associations with the noted firms of Omni Environmental Corporation, Jacobs Environmental, Inc., and Dames & Moore. His public sector, environmental experience includes serving as Manager of Air Quality for the Arizona Department of Environmental Quality, and Research Scientist for the New Jersey Department of Environmental Protection. Dr. Soporowski is a veteran high school science teacher and athletic coach. In an administrative capacity, he served as Director of Science, Music, Art, and Alternative Programs for a New Jersey Public School System where he was also responsible for developing and implementing the district's Science, Technology, Engineering, and Mathematics Program.

Joseph J. Soporowski, Ph.D.
Director, Academic and Environmental Programs
SEA, Sustainable Education Associates, LLC
P.O. Box 398, Normandy Beach, NJ 08739
732-575-7359
seayourfuture@gmail.com
www.seayourfuture.net

Made in the USA
Middletown, DE
01 October 2023

39794525R00184